DEFIANCE
Exposing the Dark Side of the Martial Arts

DEFIANCE
Exposing the Dark Side of the Martial Arts

Bohdi Sanders, PhD

Library of Congress Cataloging-in-Publication Data
Sanders, Bohdi, 1962-
Defensive Living: The Other Side of Self-Defense

ISBN – 978-1-937884-24-6

1. Martial Arts. 3. Karate. 3. Tae Kwon Do. 4. Self-Defense.
5. MMA. 6) Kempo. 7) Kajukenbo. 8) Title.

Kaizen Quest Publishing

Acknowledgements

This book is written for all of the true martial artists out there who actually care about the future of traditional martial arts. If we all stand together, we can assure that the core values of true martial arts live on for years and years to come. But we must stand together against those who are dishonestly using the martial arts for their own gain. Together, we can conquer the dark side of the martial arts.

I want to thank Sifu Al Dacascos for his invaluable feedback and help with this book. Sifu Al is a true friend and a valued resource who is always there when I need motivation, advice, or help. I am truly blessed to be able to call Sifu Al my friend!

I also want to express my sincere appreciation to Richard Hackworth for his help with this book. Richard is like a living martial arts encyclopedia. His knowledge of the martial arts is absolutely amazing, and he freely offered his wisdom and knowledge to help with this book.

And I must thank my beautiful wife for putting up with my endless hours in my office on my computer writing my books and publishing my teachings. She has supported me since the very beginning and continues to support my teachings without end.

Table of Contents

Foreword

Wow, *DEFIANCE: Exposing the Dark Side of the Martial Arts* is definitely a page turner! I had a hard time putting it down. Most people would rather believe a beautiful lie than the ugly truth. If you are one of those who prefer to believe a beautiful lie, then don't read this book, as it states the truth!

I think that the martial arts have created more political indifferences, fake "news," and fake people, than even some of the big sports organizations, especially for a small, niche community. Without any legitimate ethical or oversight committee, the significance and ranking systems in the martial arts, regardless of style, are destined to go into a deep, dark cave with no light at the end of the tunnel.

I've been around since the early 1950's and have seen how the martial arts have evolved from a beautiful rose bud to the ugly dried up petals of today. Perhaps with this ugliness, a new way of thinking will flourish out of the mistakes of the past. But how can you move forward if you don't know the ugly truth behind beautiful lies?

The martial arts world is like the human body. If you step on a nail, every part of your body eventually feels the pain. The most natural thing to do would be to remove the nail which is causing the pain, then the whole body gets a chance to heal. But many individuals and organizations ignore the "nail," and instead of removing the nail from their foot, they just leave it in there until the whole body gets infected and eventually dies.

If you saw a baby on the freeway and a speeding Mac truck was heading towards it, would you just stand there and watch or would you try to save the baby? What would be your moral and ethical responsibility? I believe that if you are a person with any kind of integrity, you would get involved and correct the problem and not wait for somebody else to act. If not you, then who?

What Bohdi Sanders has done in *DEFIANCE: Exposing the Dark Side of the Martial Arts* is to give you a chance to understand the dark side of the martial arts. If you love the martial arts and want to see traditional martial arts values continue in the future, take this enlightening book to heart. Read it, understand it, and do something about the problems it exposes!

Bohdi has stuck his neck out to write this book and to expose the dark side of the martial arts. If you feel the same way about the problems he has brought to light, let it be heard loud and clear. You are not alone. Together we can bring traditional martial arts values, honesty, and loyalty back to the martial arts world.

I highly recommend *DEFIANCE: Exposing the Dark Side of the Martial Arts* to every martial artist, regardless of style or rank. The information in this book has needed to be stated for a long time and Bohdi Sanders had the courage to stand up against the current and write it. As Bohdi asks in this page turner, where will you stand?

Sifu Al Dacascos

Introduction

In the last few years, I have received countless emails from martial artists that have been very disillusioned by what they have seen in the martial arts community. They write about how they have witnessed many who claim to be martial arts masters and grandmasters but who conduct themselves more like sleazy conmen on Bourbon Street than true martial arts masters.

I reassure them that I have seen much of what they talk about firsthand. Having done most of my own training in a one-on-one setting with Shihan William Jackson, I guess I was a bit sheltered when it came to the dark side of the martial arts world. My own instructor, Shihan Jackson had become disillusioned with the martial arts community many years before we met at a 3-D bow shoot in the San Juan Mountains in Southwestern Colorado. So much so, that he had already left the martial arts community for the most part.

He told me how shady the political side of the martial arts were and that he wanted nothing to do with all of that anymore, but I didn't fully realize how bad it was until I experienced it personally and saw much of it for myself. Now I fully understand why he had distanced himself from organized martial arts and had become more of a loner.

Over the last several years, I have seen the dark side of the martial arts community get completely out of hand. I have met martial arts celebrities who I was honored to meet, only to later find out that they are frauds. I have seen conmen who form their own martial arts federations for no other reason than to cross-promote themselves to the rank of 10th dan and the title of grandmaster. The people who have contacted me, told me multiple stories of how they have seen the ugly, out-of-control egos of some martial artists and how these martial artists have lowered their standards and sold their honor.

They have witnessed the martial arts hall of fame scams and seen firsthand exactly how they work and how they are used by unscrupulous martial artists to market themselves. They tell me about how martial artists turn against each other like a pack of hungry wolves devouring one of their own. Unfortunately, I have also personally seen these same things.

When communicating with other martial artists about the state of the martial arts industry, we all agree that someone should stand up against this kind of activity. As a result of speaking out against their malicious and immoral activities, myself and others have been the target of some of these dishonest and vindictive martial artists who seem to be threatened by the success of others in the martial arts world.

These corrupt individuals work behind the scenes to destroy other martial artists and to attempt to control those in the martial arts world. I am constantly being contacted by others who have also seen all of this and much more, and it is truly dark and dirty! It is the dark side of the martial arts.

All of this is a side of the martial arts which, although we have all heard rumors about, it is hard to comprehend how despicable it is until you begin to experience it firsthand.

For over a decade now, many of my subscribers have asked me to write about this topic to warn others about what is going on and to help return ethics and honor to the martial arts industry. I told them that the only way I would be willing to write a book on this topic is if it did not trash the martial arts community, as those who participate in these malicious acts are in the minority.

I have been a martial artist for almost 35 years, over half of my life. I have a very deep respect for those who walk their martial path with integrity. I have earned the rank of 5th dan and know the benefits of real martial arts training. I have written several books on the martial arts philosophy and love the martial arts. I believe that everyone can benefit from the traditional martial arts training, whether they are martial artists or simply someone who wants to be able to defend himself in the streets.

True martial arts have so much to offer those who find a true master and discipline themselves to make them a part of their life. The martial arts have changed many lives for the better and have taught many the value of self-confidence, self-esteem, self-defense, good character and morals, honor, integrity, loyalty, and much more.

Yet there are many in the martial arts world who give the martial arts a bad name, people who lie, sell fake ranks and titles, libel, slander, attack others, take advantage of the naïve, destroy reputations, and use the martial arts dishonestly to con unsuspecting people. There is a whole dark side to the martial arts that most people are not aware of, at least until they stumble across it or get on the bad side of those who are a part of this sleazy illicit underworld.

To be honest, I knew that there were some people in the martial arts who were dishonest; there are people in every walk of life who are dishonest. However, I had no idea how bad it had become or how organized these people were. These people easily rival those on Wall Street who run their Ponzi schemes, as far as ruining lives and conning innocent people.

The good news is that there are a lot more true martial artists than there are fraudulent, insincere martial artists. And, if we stand together, we can take the power away from those who want to use the arts that we love in malicious and dishonest ways.

I wrote this book because I honestly do not think that most martial artists are aware of how bad the dark side of the martial arts has become. I know I wasn't aware of most of the things which I write about in this book, until I started to become known in the martial arts world. That is when many of these corrupt people started trying to weasel their way into my life, and I got a firsthand education on how these people work and how dishonest and malicious these people truly are.

Many people had mentioned some of these things to me over the last 10 years, but still, it was hard to comprehend. Some of the people that I was warned about seemed like very nice and sincere martial artists. They definitely know how to talk the talk, but so does every conman in the world. I had heard rumors about some of this stuff, but I figured that these things I was told about were very rare, especially in a community that is supposed to be based on honor, character, and integrity. I was wrong! The things I expose in this book are much more widespread than I ever could have imagined.

And what surprised me is that many martial artists seem to be aware of what these unscrupulous martial artists were doing in the martial arts world. This made me ask several questions. If people knew about these underhanded and dishonest actions, why were they not doing anything about it? Why was no one exposing them or standing up to them? Did no one really care? Are martial artists actually scared of these people?

I asked many martial arts masters these questions, and the answers were disheartening. I was told that most martial artists keep their heads down because they do not want to become the targets of these malicious people. I couldn't understand this. We are martial artists; we are supposed to have the courage to stand up against bullies and those who hurt or take advantage of the innocent.

The numerous letters and emails that I received told me that many martial artists do care about what is going on, but feel powerless to do anything about it or to stand up against it. That is, until now! This book is a call to action; and hopefully, it will give everyone who is disgusted by the corruption, lies, and the dark side of the martial arts, the motivation to stand up and say, "No more!"

While most martial artists will quickly act to help somebody who is being physically attacked, they have very little interest in coming to the aid of those who are the targets of those in the martial arts underworld. People see these attacks as simply disputes between various martial artists or a "he said, she said" scenario. Nothing could be further from the truth. True martial artists must stand together against those of low morals and malicious motives!

I was raised to never back down from a bully, for any reason. My father sat me down one day and told me that if he ever heard that I backed down from a bully, that I would get a much worse beating when I got home than any bully would have given me. And after my many run-ins with his leather belt, I had no doubt that this was true.

From that day on, I have never backed down from a bully or from someone who is abusing others. And yes, I did lose a few fights with bullies because of it. But what I learned from those fights was that, even if you lose a fight to a bully, if you hit him back hard enough and land enough punches, he never targets you again. Even in defeat, you win! And, what's more, you can walk away with your head held high, knowing that you had the courage to stand up against the bully and do the right thing.

This is how I live my life. I don't back down from bullies, conmen, thugs, liars, and the like. I simply won't do that. If you allow these people to get away with their malicious actions, they will only continue to hurt other innocent people. I don't know how any warrior or true martial artist could look himself in the mirror if he allowed that to happen. The truth is that bullies and criminals will continue their evil ways until someone finally steps up, hits them back hard, and changes their attitude.

Albert Einstein stated that, "The world is a dangerous place, not because of those who do evil, but because of those who look on and do nothing." I am not one of those people who sees evil being done and simply turns a blind eye. I never have been, and I never will be.

I believe that a true martial artist is a warrior; and warriors have a duty to serve and protect others. Warriors confront the evil that most people refuse to acknowledge. But many in the martial arts world have forgotten the way of the warrior. They see the evil and the dishonest practices going on throughout the martial arts community and simply refuse to acknowledge them.

They turn a blind eye to what is happening and pretend it doesn't affect them. If you know what is happening and are not standing up for what is right, then you are complicit in allowing these dishonest practices to continue to deteriorate the martial arts. To quote Marcus Aurelius, "You can also commit injustice by doing nothing."

If a warrior sees wrongdoings and turns a blind eye to them, how is that honorable or courageous? Cowardice has nothing to do with warriorhood. If martial artists are aware of the dishonest, deceitful, and fraudulent practices going on in the martial arts, and do nothing to stop them, who will? Someone must be willing to stand against corruption or the corruption will continue, and innocent people will continue to be fleeced and hurt by these corrupt individuals.

As I pointed out earlier, this book is not only about exposing the dark side of the martial arts, but it is a call to action for every true martial artist who cares about the future of the martial arts. It is a call to action for those who care about justice, honor, and integrity in the martial arts. It is a call to action to stand against those who take advantage of innocent people.

If you are not willing to stand against the things which are happening in the dark crevices of the martial arts world, who will? If you are not willing to get involved, why should anyone else? Warriors don't sit back and let others fight for what is right, while they watch from the sidelines and reap the benefits. Warriors don't walk the middle of the road in an attempt to stay in the good graces of both the evil and the noble. Cowards walk the middle of the road, not warriors! Warriors choose the side of justice and righteousness.

This book is also a warning for those who are new to the martial arts and those who are martial artists but do not really understand what is happening in the martial arts world. Many good students leave the martial arts disillusioned by dishonest and underhanded martial arts instructors, and many martial artists are conned and misled by these malicious people. I hope this book will serve as a guide for new students as they begin their martial arts journey and will help prevent them and others from being defrauded by another dishonest martial arts instructor.

Many have warned me that in writing this book, I will be finished in the martial arts community. They tell me that some of the people who are involved in these dishonest practices are too powerful to cross and that they will simply destroy me and my reputation.

My answer to them is, "If exposing the truth makes me an outcast in the martial arts world, then so be it. My honor is not for sale. I won't be silenced by intimidation!"

These people have already tried to silence me and destroy my reputation. They have tried everything in the book to shut me down and to cast doubts about my character in order to run me out of the martial arts world so I will stop writing my teachings and stop exposing them. They have threatened my family, my friends, and me. They have trashed my name with vicious lies. They have threatened to sue me, to come after me, and some have even threatened to "make me disappear." They have even publicly declared that they are "ending my martial arts journey."

I don't back down to bullies, conmen and frauds and neither should you. I am exposing their despicable, malicious, and deceptive actions. I am exposing the dark side of the martial arts and the chips can fall where they may. This is where I, and other martial artists of honor and high moral character, stand as far as the dark side of the martial arts is concerned. The question is, are you willing to stand with us against the dark side of the martial arts world? Where do you stand?

Bohdi Sanders

DEFIANCE

Exposing the Dark Side of the Martial Arts

武

士

道

Chapter 1
The Deterioration of the Martial Arts

Right is right, even if nobody does it.
Wrong is wrong, even if everyone is wrong about it.
G. K. Chesterton

Martial artists who have been around the martial arts world for 35 years or more know that the martial arts have really changed over the years. Back in the 1960's and 1970's, earning a black belt meant that you had paid your dues in blood, sweat, and tears. One withstood a lot of pain, injuries, struggles, disappointments, and ultimately, victory to earn that coveted prize – the black belt and all the skills and knowledge that came with it.

Early practitioners earned their black belts through hard core training. They acquired a certain skill set that they could absolutely use to inflict severe injury on others if the need arose. These people were highly disciplined and determined individuals. They were people to be revered and feared because of their spirit, dedication, training, and skills.

Today the black belt doesn't carry quite the same meaning. We see four and five-year olds wearing black belts. We see teenagers as young as 13 or 14-year-old claiming to be 4th dans (4th degree black belts). We see 18-year-old students with the title of martial arts master. The black belt has almost become a participation trophy in many dojos.

There was a time when, if someone was wearing a black belt, he had earned the rank of black belt, and it carried a certain level of respect across the board. You knew that this was someone who could, and would, defend himself. You also knew that he had the ability to really hurt you.

Unfortunately, times have changed. Do you really think that a 10-year-old black belt can defend himself against some adult predator on the streets? Do you believe that the 30-year-old martial arts "master" who has never been in a fight in his life can teach you how to defend yourself against a seasoned street fighter?

Do you believe that being able to demonstrate a certain number of katas, techniques, and showing some sparring skills in the dojo gives you the same skills as the martial arts pioneers? These pioneers brought their martial arts skills back to the United States after fighting for their lives in Asia. These military personnel were adding martial arts skills to the warrior training that they had received from the United States military.

It is time to get real about the state of the martial arts world. The martial arts have deteriorated into something that the older martial artists barely recognize today. If you compare the training that most so-called martial artists are receiving today in the United States to the training going on in Japan, China, and Korea, there is no comparison. They must look at us and laugh out loud! If you are interested in the difference, you can find many videos online which show martial arts training in Asia.

Before I go on, I want to point out that what I discuss in this chapter and throughout this book does not apply to all instructors or martial arts dojos today. There are great instructors and great dojos out there where you can still get hard core, old school training, although these are becoming fewer and far between. I have been blessed to meet and to get to know many great martial artists for whom I have great respect.

I have met many more whom I have very little or no respect. They are actively using the martial arts for nothing more than personal gain (and I am not referring to self-improvement), much like a body building gym or yoga studio. Unlike the gym or yoga studio, they are promising their students things which they do not, and cannot, deliver. This is where the problem lies.

Not everyone can teach martial arts in a way that prepares students in the art of self-defense. They may be able to teach them some rote techniques or to memorize certain katas or forms. They may even be able to teach them how to win a few trophies at a tournament here and there. They can teach them how to scream at the top of their lungs (I will address this in a later chapter). But they are not teaching their students true martial arts.

To many, learning a few blocks, kicks, punches, katas, and some flashy weapon routines for the tournaments *is* martial arts. But the true martial artist knows that all of that is almost worthless without knowing how and when to use these things for self-defense, when and when not to fight, de-escalation techniques, character training, and much more.

The hobbyist does martial arts; the true martial artist lives the warrior lifestyle. There is a huge difference! One is a game or a fun hobby, and the other is a way of the warrior, a way of life. The way of the warrior entails more than going to class two nights a week and the occasional tournament. It entails more than participating in another hobby or fun activity.

The gymnastic moves you now see at the martial arts tournaments, along with the obnoxious screaming which passes for kiais, are not true martial arts and are almost totally worthless as far as self-defense goes. These "Hollywood" ideas of the martial arts may be cool to watch in the tournaments, but they are not real martial arts, at least not in the traditional sense.

A baton twirler can spin her baton and kick her legs up high. Cheerleaders can do high kicks, and gymnasts can do flips all over the mats, but none of that makes any of them martial artists. In the same manner, fancy spinning bo staff techniques and screaming fake kiais do not make sports participants true martial artists. These are just shadows of true martial arts.

True martial arts involve so much more than learning how to fight or how to do certain katas or forms. Learning how to fight is a very important part of being a martial artist. Self-defense is one of the main reasons that most people start martial arts classes in the first place. Most of these people simply assume that the instructor wearing that impressive black belt knows what he is doing, but this assumption is increasingly not the case.

Many martial arts instructors today have never been in a real fight of any kind, much less a life-or-death situation. Most have never even been punched in the face. They may have been hit a few times with large padded gloves in the dojo while wearing head gear or in a tournament where drawing a drop of blood, or even hitting a little too hard, gets you disqualified.

However, they have never been hit by a seasoned street thug determined to send them to the hospital or worse. I can assure you, there is a huge difference between taking a punch in the dojo and taking a punch by someone who truly wants to hurt you.

They have never faced down an attacker wielding a knife or a club. They don't know what it is like to be beat to a pulp and left for dead. They have never felt the adrenalin rush or the tunnel vision that you get when attacked by someone who is intent on hurting or killing them. In short, they have no idea what true self-defense is, what it entails, or what it is like to fight for your life.

And no, I am not saying that every true martial artist must have these experiences. But, if you are going to teach students who want to learn how to defend themselves in such circumstances, it is necessary to understand these kinds of attacks and the mental and physical aspects which accompany a physical attack, which many instructors today do not understand.

Our culture in today's world has changed. When I was growing up, most boys learned how to fight either at school or in the streets, at least to some degree. Today, even if a boy is defending himself against some bully who attacks him at school, the infinite wisdom of our inept school administrators dictates that the boy should be suspended and given the same punishment as the attacker/bully. This is idiotic!

These lethargic administrators proudly brag about their "no tolerance policy" against violence. But not only does this "no tolerance policy" rob the good boys and girls from learning how to defend themselves, it is simply un-American and wrong! It teaches our boys and girls that it is wrong to defend themselves and that one should always look to an authority figure to fight their battles for them. It teaches them not to be independent and strong, but to depend on the state. What a bunch of crap that is!

Before I ever set foot in an actual dojo, I already knew how to fight. I had been in countless street fights and bar fights. Some were very serious, and some were merely boys being boys. I had already experienced several knives being pulled on me, been shot at, been beat and left for dead, and had been attacked with several make-shift weapons over the years. I had also put several guys in the hospital, which is not something I like to brag about, but it's simply the truth.

When I started training in martial arts, I wanted to learn martial arts to become a better fighter so I could take people down quicker and feel undefeatable. I wanted to be able to walk into a bar and know for a fact that I was the most dangerous person there. Of course, this was silly and immature, but it was where my mind was at the time. After starting karate, I quickly learned how ridiculous those ideas were.

I dove into the martial arts, learning more about the reality of fighting and how easy it is to badly injure the human body. I learned the importance of philosophy, character training, and only fighting when you have no other choice. I quit getting in all those unnecessary or ridiculous fights. I quit going out looking for trouble and started avoiding trouble as much as I could.

I was lucky enough to accidentally step into a dojo with an experienced instructor who had lived and trained in Japan. I learned the true meaning of discipline and what it means to take your martial arts training seriously. I was fortunate to have started martial arts before they started deteriorating into what they have largely become today, and my life is better for it.

Today one would be hard-pressed to find many students with my background of street fighting, which is not necessarily a bad thing. Most students are either looking for self-defense training because of something bad which has happened to them, or they simply think martial arts is cool and want to learn all the flashy martial arts moves like they see on television and the movies. There are quite a few instructors who can teach the flashy "play" stuff; there are few who can teach the whole package – the warrior lifestyle.

I used to be a schoolteacher until I simply could not stand the politically correct garbage which is going on in today's school system. I cannot tell you how many times martial arts trolls on social media have attacked me saying, "Bohdi is not a martial arts master; he is an ex-schoolteacher." These people never cease to expose their ignorance of the martial arts. I guess it slipped their minds that Master Gichin Funakoshi, founder of Shotokan Karate, was also a schoolteacher. Master Funakoshi taught martial arts on the side and not as a full-time job, at least not at first.

One of Master Funakoshi's most well-known quotes is, "The ultimate aim of karate lies not in victory or defeat, but in the perfection of character of its participants." True martial arts encompass much more than learning a few techniques, rank promotions, and how to spar. True martial artists must work to perfect their martial arts skills, self-defense skills, and work to perfect their character at the same time.

I have seen many "martial artists" say things like, "I am not interested in all that philosophy stuff. I am just a down and dirty fighter." They get one thing right; they are *just* a down and dirty fighter and not a martial artist. If you want to be a real martial artist, you must work to perfect your character as well as your physical martial arts skills. Teaching a student to develop all the dangerous skills, without teaching them the character, honor, morals, and the spiritual side of the arts to go along with them, is simply training a dangerous thug, period.

I wonder what Master Funakoshi and the other founding fathers of the martial arts would think of statements such as, "I am not interested in the philosophy and character training." I also wonder what the old masters would think of the mixed martial arts with all the trash talking and emphasis on nothing more than fighting in a cage. It seems that the martial arts have gone to the extreme in several different directions, many which have forgotten that true

6

martial arts are about being a balanced, complete person, not simply about fighting or winning trophies.

If you look back at the old teachings, the original masters all taught the importance of developing good character in your martial arts students. This was so important to them that they were very selective about who they would and would not take on as students. They absolutely would not teach just anyone who walked through their door and requested instruction.

Today, most martial arts instructors will teach anyone and everyone who has the money to pay them, which brings me to why there has been such a deterioration of the martial arts. The martial arts community in our culture today revolves around one thing for the most part – MONEY.

I actually had a woman who has been inducted into many so-called "martial arts halls of fame," tell me, "Everybody in the martial arts world are in competition with each other. There is only so much money to go around in the martial arts world, and we are all fighting to get our share." This is such a sickening statement coming from a so-called "martial arts hall of fame inductee."

I later found out that this woman is not even a martial artist. She was given an "honorary black belt" for running a couple of cheesy martial arts websites which she runs for her own personal financial gain, making money from Google ads. That is her only claim to fame in the martial arts world and apparently was enough to get her "inducted" into several "halls of fame." But I will address these martial arts hall of fame scams in a later chapter.

I think it would be hard to find serious martial artists who would disagree that the martial arts world has declined from what it once was. The training has lost the very essence of what the martial arts were originally meant to be – spiritually, mentally, and physically. It is now hyper-focused on sports, on tournaments and winning trophies, on cage fighting, or on simply being a fun hobby for everyone. True martial arts instruction has become harder and harder to find in today's martial arts world.

It has become increasingly more difficult to find a martial arts instructor who is willing to integrate all the components of complete martial arts training in their classes for one reason or another. Either they do not know much about these things themselves because they were never taught them, or they don't want to risk offending the parents of their students, consequently costing themselves income.

Others are just plain not interested in teaching things such as character training, hard core self-defense, meditation, etc. and prefer to focus solely on the sports aspect of the arts. The justifications are endless, but the results are the same – we are losing the true spirit of the martial arts. No matter what the reasons may be, it is evident that the martial arts world is losing its true essence.

We have entirely too many people who call themselves "martial artists" but who couldn't care less about true martial arts or what the martial arts are meant to be. These people are mainly interested in putting more money in their pockets and maintaining their own façade in order to continue to fleece others or to promote themselves through questionable means. Their egos are totally out of control and guide their actions.

The old ways are not good enough for them. Character, honor, and integrity are only terms which they use to market their dojo to potential students. They start their own federations for personal gain and to be able to promote themselves to ranks and titles that they are either too lazy or too impatient to earn. They start fake martial arts halls of fame to pamper their egos and the egos of their fake friends, as well as, to put thousands of dollars in their pockets. They give themselves and their so-called "friends" unearned rank like they are passing out candy at Halloween.

Many of these people sell rank and titles like they are flipping used cars. And if they can't find somewhere to buy their martial arts ranks, they simply promote themselves to a high rank through fraudulent means using today's technology which enables them to con unsuspecting people. They have given up the old ways and sold their martial arts soul (if they ever had one) for entertainment and minor celebrity status in a small niche community.

8

Too many so-called martial artists have sold their honor and integrity for fame, fortune, and to stroke their own overblown and fragile egos. They gossip, backbite, and attack each other with hateful rhetoric through the most dishonest of ways. Humility, respect and honor have been replaced with egotistical pride, bragging, and outright lies and fraud.

Instead of using today's technology to bring martial artists together as one, they use technology and gossip as a weapon to destroy the reputations of other martial artists in a misguided attempt to advance and market themselves, instead of working to earn true respect. These are all aspects of the dark side of today's martial arts world.

This chapter is a general overview of how the martial arts world is changing in our modern Western culture. I will get deeper into the specific ways in which the martial arts world is deteriorating in the following chapters. There are many unscrupulous people in the martial arts community who are doing many unethical things to market themselves to students and parents, or to simply cash in on the popularity of the martial arts.

Hopefully, by the time you finish this book, you will have a much better understanding about what the martial arts are meant to be versus what they have become. I present many red flags to watch for when searching for good quality martial arts training, the many ways corrupt martial artists take advantage of others for their own personal gain, and I also offer many solutions to stop the deterioration of the martial arts.

The Bible states that the *love* of money is the root of all evil. And if you start to delve into what has happened to the martial arts world, you can see that the deterioration of the martial arts is directly connected to the *love* of money. One can trace the majority of the current problems in the martial arts community back to this one evil which causes so much pain in our world – the *love* of money.

In the next chapter, I will discuss some of the ways unscrupulous "martial artists" sell their honor and integrity to satisfy their never-ending lust for money. Some of them are more common than others, but they all stem from the dark side of human nature and contribute to the deterioration of the martial arts world.

To return to the root is to find the meaning,
but to pursue appearances is to miss the source.
Seng Ts'an

Chapter 2
Show me the MONEY!

Few men have the virtue to withstand the highest bidder.
George Washington

Much of the martial arts world now revolves around the almighty dollar. From long term contracts that rope parents and students into long term monthly payments, even if their child changes his mind about martial arts, to ridiculous fees for rank promotion, to outright selling of rank and titles, it is undeniable that a lot of today's martial arts world revolves around money.

In this chapter I am going to delve into some of the money-making scams which are common across the martial arts world. Again, I want to emphasize that not all dojos or instructors participate in these questionable activities, but many of them do. You have to do your due diligence in order to make sure you are getting quality training and not simply getting ripped off.

Let's start by looking at a real example of a McDojo with questionable practices. There is a McDojo outside of the San Jose, CA area which is located in a small strip mall. At first glance, this place actually looks legitimate. They have a nice website with rotating photos of the instructor with famous martial artists. The walls of this dojo are covered with photos of this instructor with well-known martial artists which are meant to give the impression that he is personal friends with these famous martial artists.

However, like many things in this world, the initial appearances are very deceiving; you must look below the surface to get to the truth behind the impressive looking website, all the photos of famous martial artists which cover the walls, and the false claims of this strip mall dojo.

If you were looking for a martial arts dojo for your child, you would initially be very impressed by the names this instructor drops, the photos on his walls and on his website. The whole set up looks very impressive and the instructor sells his dojo with the skills of a shady used car salesman. But there are certain facts which are cleverly hidden from the potential student or parent looking for training for his or her child.

The website has lots of impressive information and is nicely set up, but it doesn't mention the fact that this McDojo requires students to sign a long-term contract. Long-term contracts in martial arts dojos serve one purpose and one purpose only – to keep the money coming in for the instructor. This is a practice taken from the health club industry where they make most of their money from automatic payments being collected from people who were once motivated to work out, but have long since quit, yet are still locked into making monthly payments.

The martial arts instructors who use these long-term contracts fully understand that students are initially motivated to try martial arts, but that many soon lose interest and move on to other activities. This is bad for their bottom line. So what do they do? They lock their parents or students into long-term contracts while their motivation is high. After that, it doesn't matter much to them whether the student continues to train or not; the instructor still gets his monthly check for the whole term of the contract.

It is good for children to try many different sports and activities to find out what they do and do not like. Many will start a sport that they thought would be interesting, only to find out that that sport is not what they thought it would be and that they enjoy other activities more. This is simply part of being curious and wanting to try new things.

Sincere martial arts instructors understand this and are only interested in teaching those who sincerely want to learn. No honest martial arts instructor wants students in his classes who are not interested in learning martial arts anymore, but who are only there because their parents are making them come to class because they are locked into making monthly payments for the next two years. As an ex-school teacher, I can attest to how miserable it is to try to teach when you have students who have no interest in learning.

Since this chapter is not about debating the merits of whether or not parents should require a child to follow through if they start a sport or activity, I won't get into the pros and cons of the "finish what you start" philosophy. That is an individual parenting decision which should be left up to the parents. That said, the parents should actually have the choice about making this decision.

The truth is that many children quit the martial arts out of boredom because the classes are being taught by unqualified school owners who just run a "martial arts" themed exercise/workout program with very little actual self-defense, philosophy, history, or character being taught. In this case, the child does not want to quit because they are "lazy or weak," as many instructors will insist. But rather, it is that they lose interest because the instructor's classes didn't capture the attention of the child or didn't fulfill the promises of the school's false marketing campaign.

In this Tae Kwon Do McDojo in California, apparently the instructor disagrees with this philosophy. Like many McDojos, this one ropes students and parents into long-term contracts by making promises which, according to the reviews of this dojo by parents and students, are rarely kept. Here are some of the actual reviews of this dojo from students and parents from Yelp. These reviews will give you an idea of some of the things you should watch out for when trying to find a martial arts dojo for yourself or your children.

* "I think I owe it to everyone in town to share my horrible experience with XXXX and Master X. He agreed to create a small class for a group of kindergartners who wanted to join his studio. He was always late or sometimes would not even show up for our class without any notice or even apologies. After tolerating him for more than a year, we were fed up with his lack of respect for us as customers and decided that it was time for us to choose another activity for the boys. We all informed him a couple of weeks in advance, and he confirmed it by email. After we stopped going to his studio, he kept on charging all of us (4 families). We tried to communicate the issue with him through emails and phone calls, but he totally ignored all of us. We decided to file a dispute with our credit card company. To our surprise and wonder, he had tried to reverse our dispute with false claims. When each one of us received the documents from our credit card companies, we were SPEECHLESS. [He went to] so much trouble of making up paperwork to show false attendance and a totally made-up contract. I was so upset, and so were the other 3 moms!! I had to spend hours to go through old emails, and find bits and pieces to show he was lying!! I got my money back, but

my friends are still in the process of their claims with their credit card companies. We sent him an email, saying that we will write a review for him, and all of a sudden, he started replying to us. He said his accountant might have made a mistake, and why did not we communicate with him, and that he needed a few days to sort things out and he will return our money. A month later, when my friends followed up with him, he said that he has a no return policy and he does not like drama. This guy is unbelievable!!"

* "They work hard to get you in and once you are in their fold and they figure you are not going elsewhere, the quality just drops! And from what I've experienced, [the] fleecing begins. My kids really miss 'learning' tae-kwon-do since they've joined this studio. They now feel like it simply is a 45 minute daycare activity. Quite a few other parents are stuck likewise, as they've paid for a few months in advance. So the warning is – never, never pay up in advance…a lot of young kids are going to this studio and older ones are not to be seen...go figure."

* "If you love used car salesmen, you might love these guys. We went in to look around, and they pounced. I felt like the time I accidentally set foot in a used car lot. Afterward, we got a call every single day for five days, asking us when we were going to come in and give them the $500 they want. No, "try it for a month and see if you like it" here. Nope, it's "drop $500, and if you don't like it, we'll keep the money. You can keep the spiffy white suit, which by the way costs $60. Well, they don't say that quite so blatantly. But they do make sure you sign something that says "no refunds." I decided never to join the class after the second phone call. Save yourself the spam, give them a false number."

* "Billing was an issue. When I had questions, Master X. said I had to talk to his billing company because he had NO CONTROL over billing (he said this multiple times). As a business owner, if you do not have control, you do not own the business. At the start we signed up for monthly lessons. Two months down the road, I was asked to get another signed contract because he did not have a copy. We made the mistake of not reading the contract thinking it was the same as the original. It was not... Master X. told me he had "NO CONTROL OVER BILLING AND THERE ARE NO REFUNDS."

* "My son, 6 years old and four of his friends, attended class with Master X. for almost a year. As for his instruction, Master X. did belittle the children if they were late to class, had to go to the bathroom, etc. I understand trying to instill discipline and respect in the children, but you have to practice what you preach. Master X was continuously late himself and on occasion would not show up for class without any notice… As for his business practice and professionalism, watch out. He continued to charge us after we cancelled the class. I received an email from him confirming that our auto pay would stop. When the billing continued, I called and emailed him several times to resolve the issue. When I did not receive an answer, I went to my credit card company to dispute the charge. He submitted documents showing an attendance record that showed my son in class for 3 months when he had not been."

14

* "If I had the option to provide a negative star I would. Brought my kids there for over a year and when they lost interest and we wanted to cancel, all of the sudden we were the bad people. He tried everything to take our money and threatened reporting us to the credit bureau. He lies about his accounting practices and has a fake accountant that is him responding to accounting questions. He deletes all negative feedback. Do some digging on Facebook and Yelp and you'll see a list of people complaining about the same problems. As long as you're there and paying, everything is fine. The moment you want to leave, Master X. is a different person."

* "I reviewed XXXX a while back but removed the review because Master X. kept emailing me saying my review was wrong. I was done with being harassed with emails... I'm back to share my family's experience. Most people have already written about X.'s attitude and arrogance, his inattention to how the kids are feeling or experiencing during the class, the act of being interested and encouraging only up until you sign on and pay. My son never felt encouragement in the class, but he was embarrassed publicly by X. a few times, until he refused to ever go back there. I couldn't blame my son for wanting to quit, but the sad thing is, he says he never wants to try another martial art again. I hope that will one day change because he loved doing martial arts."

These are just a sample of some of the reviews from Yelp for this McDojo outside of San Jose, CA; there are many more. But this gives you a pretty good idea about how some of the shadier martial arts instructors do business. Just like the used car salesman, these conmen are smooth talkers and will promise you the world, that is, until you sign on the dotted line. Then the nightmare begins!

That said, not all martial arts contracts are bad. A good contract should serve to protect *both* parties, not just the martial arts instructor. Make sure you read any contract you sign very closely and if you have any issues with any part of it, discuss them with the instructor. Also, make sure you get any promises or changes *in writing*. I would also insist on an exit clause in case you or your student decide to leave the dojo later.

If the instructor is involved in shady practices, you can be fairly sure that the contract is set up to his advantage and that he will not be flexible or work with you down the line, just like so many parents found out with this hack in California. It is up to you to be smart and watch out for these conmen, and have no doubt about it, the martial arts world is full of sleazy conmen and fraudulent instructors.

An honest dojo will offer you many options when it comes to payments and contracts. If the instructor at the dojo is a high-pressure salesman, like the one in the example above, do yourself a favor and go somewhere else!

True martial arts masters are not high-pressure salesmen. They are there to teach and help students develop both their character and their martial arts skills. Most real martial arts instructors are more than willing to work with both parents and students when it comes to finances and/or contracts.

When I was teaching, if a student could not afford what I was charging, I made other arrangements for them. They could earn partial scholarships in exchange for work, such as helping to clean the dojo and put up the mats, etc. after classes. I never turned away any student because he could not afford to pay. And my contracts were mostly just so both the student and/or parents and I both had a concrete understanding of what they would be learning, times, expectations, etc. They were never about roping students into any guaranteed, long-term payment plan.

Always beware of any instructor who is trying to rope you into a long-term payment contract unless you are getting a nice discount for signing up for a year or more, especially if you are not sure that the dojo or style is for you. There are a lot of clowns like "Master X." out there who will take advantage of unsuspecting parents or students who don't know much about martial arts. Buyer beware!

You should also be aware that your monthly fees do not cover things such as belt tests. Many instructors charge ridiculous fees to "test" students for their rank promotions for school ranks that are not registered with any governing body or federation. This is seen by many instructors as an additional source of income. I have seen rank promotions cost anywhere from $300 up to $1,000.

These instructors will claim that these exorbitant fees are necessary to cover the belts, the certificates, etc., but the truth is that student belts only cost around $5 or less and the certificates may only cost $1 or a little more, depending on the specific situation. The exception to this is when instructors belong to a worldwide organization that offers rank registration which allows for the student's rank to be recognized should he or she move and go to another school from that same style. These obviously cost more.

Belt testing in many dojos is done in a group setting, not an individual one-on-one setting; and in some dojos, is done every two or three months for students under the rank of black belt. Every dojo sets their own standards and timelines. There is no standard across the board for all martial arts.

However, when students and the school belong to a worldwide federation or governing body, the school must follow a standardized curriculum where students of each level learn the same things from school to school much like the standards in public education. If you move to another city in your state, then your child should be able to start training in the new city at the same level they were at the old school. This is one of the benefits of standardization.

On the other hand, many independent schools do not follow such standards and their rank fees are simply ways for the school owner to pad his own back account. For example, if the dojo has 50 students and charges $100 for belt tests every three months, that is an extra $5,000 every three months, minus a small amount for the belts and certificates. That is a nice bonus every quarter! Not to mention, an unexpected expense for the students or parents.

When I started my martial arts journey, I was in a dojo that required all students to be a member of the JKA, Japanese Karate Association. There was a fee for the membership and the federation also got a cut of the fees for rank promotions. The costs for belt tests were around $300. And that was in the 1980's when $300 was a lot of money!

There are hundreds of "ghost" federations throughout the martial arts world which are actually owned by the school owners without any branch member schools anywhere else. Many of these federations are just as shady as the instructor from California, and are guilty of selling belt ranks, titles, and of something called cross-promotions, which I will discuss in a later chapter. Always make sure you ask about these hidden costs when signing up for martial arts training. For people on a tight budget, these hidden costs may come as quite a shock if they are expecting them to be included in their monthly fees.

Also, it should be a red flag for you if no one ever *fails* a belt test. Tests are to evaluate your level of knowledge, skill, and learning; and just like in the classroom of every school, some students make "A's" and some students fail the test. If every student always passes the test with flying colors, something should feel a little off to you. The one exception to this would be if the instructor does not allow a student to test if he is not ready. This is something that many instructors will do.

Belt testing under a qualified instructor usually comes after a few pre-tests to prepare the student for the actual test. But, if a school has testing every three months and every student gets a rank promotion at every test, this is more like a participation trophy than an actual belt test. Students should *earn* their rank promotions; it shouldn't be some automatic award just for showing up and paying for the test.

A large part of martial arts training is developing a student's character. That is done by giving the student the opportunity to *earn* each of his or her ranks, not by *giving* them a new rank every three months, six months, or whatever. When a student works to *earn* his rank through dedication and hard work, the student will feel good about himself and will develop an improved sense of self-confidence.

If he is simply *given* a rank promotion every three to six months, it doesn't carry the same meaning or value to him. And make no mistake, the student knows whether or not he is earning his rank or if it is simply being given to him.

An honorable instructor will be fair with rank promotions. If a student fails, the instructor will use the test as a teaching opportunity, correcting what the student did wrong and letting him

18

know what he needs to work on to achieve the specific rank. It is fraudulent to promote a student to a rank which he hasn't earned, and this practice gives the student a false sense of his abilities, which could get the student hurt if he believes his skills are at a level which they are not.

A couple of the reviews of the McDojo used as examples in this chapter, mentioned that after the initiation period, the dojo became more of a daycare environment than actual martial arts training. One parent stated, "They now feel like it simply is a 45 minute daycare activity." I have found that this is also very common in many *unscrupulous* dojos, especially ones where the instructor has questionable skills and/or rank himself.

I have seen "dojos" where the students were running around playing Nerf wars, shooting Nerf guns at each other, playing tag, just plain goofing off, or even playing video games. Personally, I would be irate if I were paying $100-$150 a month for my son to learn martial arts, and I walked in and he was playing Nerf wars with Nerf guns or sitting in front of a screen playing video games!

This has absolutely nothing to do with martial arts training. It is these kinds of things that give the martial arts world a bad name. You find these time fillers in dojos where the instructor is more concerned about making money than actually training students. In my book, this is someone who is not doing his job and that is totally unacceptable!

If you were paying a guy $100 a month to mow your lawn once a week, and he decided to relax on your deck instead, you would not keep paying him. You would fire him immediately as he was not giving you the service that you paid for. Why would you put up with a martial arts instructor who is simply babysitting when you are paying him to actually *teach your child* martial arts? Yet, many parents do just that.

You don't see this kind of garbage in adult classes, as adults would never put up with paying for instruction and not getting what they paid for. But many parents drop their kids off at karate and come back to pick them up, giving these unscrupulous instructors the chance to simply take a break from teaching and let the kids play games instead.

If you are a parent looking to get your children into a martial arts dojo, I would highly recommend that you do some research into how children are trained in martial arts in Japan, China, or Korea. I can promise you; you won't see them playing Nerf wars or tag. You will see some young kids doing some amazing martial arts katas, techniques, etc. and with amazing discipline.

Why should you expect less for your children? You are paying for a service, for professional martial arts training for your children; why would you settle for someone giving you nothing more than a glorified babysitting service? These practices are all too common at martial arts schools that run summer camps or after school programs.

If you want your child in an actual martial arts program and want to avoid "martial arts themed" daycare, then be on the lookout for "homework" rooms that also have video game systems set up in them or big screen televisions and DVD players where they use movie time as a way to fill the day while the instructor does nothing.

Another unprincipled way that some instructors sell their honor for money is selling rank and titles. Many will outright sell a student a certain rank or title, complete with a belt and certificate. You would be absolutely shocked to see how much some people are willing to pay for a martial arts rank that they have not earned. Some so-called martial artists will pay thousands of dollars to be promoted to an advanced rank.

They then use their purchased rank to market themselves to unsuspecting students, calling themselves martial arts "masters" or even "grandmasters." Students who are unfamiliar with the martial arts world do not know enough to question the instructor about how or where he got his rank. After all, the instructor has the certificate and fancy black belt to go with his title, he must be legitimate, right? Wrong!

Unless you know something about martial arts or know people who do, it is almost impossible for a beginning student to figure out that this guy is a complete fraud. Does this sound like a scam to you? Good! It should. And this happens much more often than you might think. I have seen guys stating that they have 30 or 40 10th degree black belts, and even one guy who claimed he had 50 10th degree black belts in various styles! It is absolutely ridiculous!

While this may sound impressive to someone who doesn't know anything about martial arts, those who have even basic martial arts knowledge know that these people are nothing more than con artists who are lying about their background in order to bilk unsuspecting people out of their money. The *love* of money truly is the root of all evil.

If you are serious about finding a good martial arts instructor, do your homework. You should know by now that anyone can write anything on the internet, so don't believe things on the internet unless you can verify them from people you know you can trust.

It is best to find a knowledgable martial artist that you trust and get his or her advice. Older martial artists who have been around for a while often know many people and can tell you who is legitimate and who is not. The martial arts world is a fairly small community, and many of the frauds are fairly well-known. A good school that uses a quality curriculum is highly organized with monthly calendars of training and events.

One caveat, beware when it comes to who you get your advice from when it comes to martial artists. The martial arts world is full of cliques. If you are speaking to someone with a grudge towards another martial artist, he may give you false information simply because he doesn't like the guy or because he is not a part of his organization. It is dirty business, but it happens all the time in the martial arts. I will be discussing this in detail in a future chapter, so I won't get into it at this time.

I hope that you have learned from this chapter that choosing a martial arts instructor or dojo is not nearly as simple as seeing a sign on the street, walking in, talking to the instructor for a few minutes, and signing up. More often than not that will leave you disillusioned.

It takes time and effort to find a good instructor and a trustworthy dojo. You must do some research and do your homework. If you are serious about learning a quality martial art from a true martial arts master, you have to do a lot of digging. Don't take anything at face value.

In today's world, it is all too easy for people to buy a black belt, print out a certificate on the computer, go to some martial arts events and take photos with real martial artists, and then present themselves as real martial arts masters. This is done all the time in the martial arts world and is something that most people who are not familiar with the martial arts do not know about.

Even many martial artists are shocked when they find out how widespread these underhanded practices are. I have been practicing martial arts for over 34 years now, and I am still shocked by some of the stories and frauds that I am made aware of, not to mention the ones I have crossed paths with personally. These people have no shame and will take you to the cleaners if you are not careful when it comes to choosing an instructor.

Just be aware that there are people in this world, in every walk of life, who will do all sorts of underhanded things for the love of money. The martial arts world is no different than any other community; there are people in every profession who are willing to lie, cheat, and steal if it will put more money in their pockets.

The love of money and poor character has caused many martial artists to sell their honor for a few dollars. As the old saying goes, if you are willing to sell your honor, you will always find a buyer.

The martial arts world has become big business and many instructors are willing to lower their standards in order to compete for more students. You must be aware of this and be very careful when looking for the right martial arts instructor.

There are many wonderful, dedicated, knowledgable, and honorable martial arts instructors out there, and there are also many unscrupulous martial arts instructors like the one in my example at the beginning of this chapter. Reputable martial arts instructors love their art much more than they love money. They are more interested in helping students and fostering the martial arts than they are in getting rich by teaching martial arts.

Money has changed the martial arts world across the board. From tournaments, which are more like gymnastic spectacles, to selling everything imaginable to the martial arts enthusiast, martial arts has become big business. Everywhere you look, there is another martial arts hall of fame popping up that is willing to give martial artists a "hall of fame" award as long as they send them a couple hundred dollars.

While it has become easier to find a martial arts dojo (they are everywhere), it has gotten much harder to find a true martial arts master. This happens in part because the martial arts industry is unregulated. That means that anyone can get a business license, rent a building, hang a sign, claim to be a master, and teach to the public. Many unqualified and unscrupulous people are taking advantage of the fact that the martial arts are totally unregulated.

Wherever there is an opportunity to make money, you will find dishonest people who will pretty much do anything to get their hands on your money. It is totally up to you, the student or the parent, to make sure that you find an instructor who is qualified, honest, loves his art, has the experience and knowledge to teach you what you want to learn, and has real credentials. And that is much harder than it may sound.

The vast majority of martial arts instructors, which I have a lot of respect for, do not teach martial arts as their main source of income. They have jobs such as schoolteachers, real estate agents, construction workers, etc. You will find these martial arts masters in almost every walk of life. They are teaching martial arts in their spare time or after work because they love their art and want to share it with students who want to learn.

Beware of those who do nothing but martial arts for a living. This is not to say that if someone does teach martial arts for a living that he or she is not on the up and up. It is never wise to generalize, as there are no hard and fast rules when it comes to what you do for a living. I happen to know several honest martial arts masters who actually do teach martial arts for a living. I am simply urging you to be careful and do your homework. Not everything is as it first appears; just ask the parents who sent their students to "Master X." to learn martial arts!

In this chapter, I have used the term "McDojo" several times when referring to the strip mall dojo in California and other dojos which are more concerned with making money than actually teaching martial arts. In the next chapter, I will get into what this term means and how to distinguish between a McDojo and a true dojo.

The true meaning of Budo was lost.
I see a lot of people talking about training
in martial arts, however, when one looks closely
inside, there is no substance to what they are doing.
Sekiguchi Takaaki

Chapter 3
McDojos

Things are not always what they seem;
the first appearance deceives many;
the intelligence of the few perceives
what has been carefully hidden.
Plato

To begin this chapter, I first need to define what a McDojo is. A McDojo refers to a martial arts dojo which is more focused on making money and marketing, than on truly teaching students the way of the warrior. Instructors in these "dojos" are not honestly invested in their students; rather they are invested in making a name for themselves, getting as many students as they can, roping them into long-term contracts, and making as much money as possible.

The majority of students in a McDojo will be young kids and instead of teaching these young students a good foundation in the martial arts, the classes are mostly based around fun activities for the kids. The students are given rank promotions fairly often in order to keep them motivated and keep their parents paying for their lessons.

The parents wrongly assume that their children are "advancing," as evidenced by the new stripe on little Johnny's belt or the new color belt Suzy just received. Since most parents do not know much about the martial arts, it makes it easy for these unscrupulous instructors to give the impression that little Johnny or Suzy is quickly advancing towards their black belt. Little do they know that these McDojos use rank promotion, stripes, etc., as a way to keep their students, and their parents, motivated to continue coming to their dojo.

They prey on unsuspecting soccer moms and other parents who know little about the martial arts or how to choose a good martial arts dojo. Often times, parents put their children in these classes to learn self-defense because they have been bullied at school, thinking that they will learn how to defend themselves. But true self-defense is rarely taught in a McDojo, however, the parents have no way of knowing this and are simply being fleeced.

These McDojos also prey on the insecure, alpha male type guys who find the quick rank promotions very attractive. These guys are not truly interested in the martial arts lifestyle, but rather, they simply want to get a black belt in order to feel good about themselves or for bragging rights to impress others about how tough they are. They are promised a black belt in a year or two, which is very attractive to guys who are more interested in appearances than they are in training.

McDojos are also called belt mills or paper mills. They give out belt rank advancements like participation trophies, and along with the new belt comes a fancy certificate "proving" how much of a badass little Johnny has become.

These dojos usually market themselves as teaching practical self-defense, which is potentially "deadly" or "unstoppable." I have news for you, there is no martial art which is unstoppable, and a hammer or a screwdriver are both "potentially deadly." These dojos also market themselves as teaching discipline to their students. When parents watch a class, they see kids bowing and saying, "Yes sir and no sir." This gives the parents the impression that their kids are truly learning respect and discipline, when in fact, these dojos are simply going through the motions with very little true principles.

Parents and potential martial arts students need to understand that anyone, anywhere can claim to be a martial arts master or grandmaster of some 800-year-old martial art. There are no universally set standards which govern the martial arts world. Thus, fakes and frauds abound in the martial arts community, and it can be almost impossible for even seasoned martial artists to know who is legitimate and who is a fraud.

Each individual martial arts master can award belt rank according to their own subjective terms. Many times, this means that they award belt rank and titles according to friendship, loyalty, and of course, money. I have seen many fraudulent martial arts masters who have awarded their friends belt rank for no other reason than they are friends. I have also heard of many who sell rank for thousands of dollars.

26

Since the martial arts world is unregulated, it gives dishonest martial arts instructors the perfect opportunity to use such underhanded practices to build up their reputation by awarding, or selling, black belts to people and then using those same people to market their dojo. You will hear them brag about how many black belts they have under them.

McDojos are also where you will see a much larger focus on tournaments and winning trophies than on hard core training. Many of these dojos will require the students to keep their trophies in the dojo, where they are used to impress potential students and parents. The trophies are used as visual marketing aids and are a source of free marketing for the instructor.

In these dojos you can see the new trend of the traditional kiai being replaced by obnoxiously loud, and long, screaming. The Japanese term, "kiai," is a combination of two Japanese characters. "Ki" means life force and "Ai" means to blend or harmonize. When combined, kiai literally means to concentrate your life force.

Kiai is also known as the spirit shout in some circles. I guess some cheesy McDojo instructor figured that the louder the spirit shout is, the better it is. Now, in almost every tournament, traditional kiais, especially in katas and forms, have been replaced by the students screaming as loud and as long as possible, which is simply silly, not to mention loathsome.

I wonder what these guys would think if they actually knew that in many martial arts, the kiai is completely silent. You don't have to scream and shout to focus your energy or your ki into your technique, as evidenced by arts such as Kenjutsu where the energy is focused and transferred through the blades. This is just another example of these McDojos going through the motions without a true understanding of the meaning behind the techniques.

As I stated, you will see a huge focus on tournaments and winning trophies in these McDojos. This is not to say that every dojo that competes in tournaments is a McDojo. That would be completely incorrect. Tournaments absolutely have their place in the martial arts world. It is the obsessive focus on winning and competing that is the difference.

On the other hand, the tournaments hardly resemble true martial arts anymore. They appear more like flashy gymnastics shows and modern entertainment programs more than traditional martial arts tournaments. And while they are definitely fun to watch and entertaining, they have little in common with traditional martial arts.

In addition, the judging in many of the local tournaments is set up to favor the host dojo, assuring that the local dojo gets plenty of marketing from the event and lots of new trophies in which to market their dojo to prospective students. I have been to tournaments where a student performs a kata perfectly, but the judges dock him points because "that is not the way we perform the kata here."

Tournaments have also become nothing more than a shadow of what they used to be, as far as the sparring events go. You can be disqualified if your technique is seen as "too hard" or if you draw blood in any way. Compare these tournament rules with what you see in Asia, and it will appear that you are watching two different arts!

Sparring use to be seen as a way to practice your self-defense skills. And sparring in the tournaments use to be a way of testing your skills with other martial artists. However, in many of these schools today, sparring has simply become a game of tag and has next to nothing to do with actual self-defense skills. In fact, the closer your attacks get towards self-defense techniques, the more likely you are to be disqualified in today's martial arts tournaments.

In addition, I used to never see a martial artist act disrespectfully at tournaments, not towards other martial artists and definitely not towards any of the black belts who were judging the competitions. The martial artists competed and afterwards would bow and shake hands in a show of mutual respect. Today, I have seen Tae Kwon Do competitors scream at the judges, throw chairs, spit at their opponents, and simply throw little hissy fits when they don't win or

28

disagree with the judges. Whatever happened to martial arts beginning and ending with respect?

Another shady practice among these McDojos is the "making" of so-called "world champions." I have seen more and more martial artists claiming to be world champions. I have seen so many that one might wonder, how can there truly be that many world champions.

The truth is that most so-called "world champions" are not really world champions at all. To be a recognized world champion, one must compete in a ladder tournament system. Here is an example of how a ladder tournament system works.

First, you would need to be selected by your instructor to represent your school at a local city or county level tournament. If you win there, you will advance to a district level tournament. Those winners advance to the state championships. The winners at the state level are appointed to the state team to represent their home state at the national championships.

Those who win at the national competition are then invited to national team tryouts. If they are selected by the national team coaches, then they are appointed to the national team that will represent their country at a world championship for that year. If they win, they are considered a recognized world champion.

Here is the twist. There are organizations that sanction tournaments for a fee. If you pay a high enough fee, you can host a "World Ranked Tournament" and the winners of your event are then called "World Champions." The largest of these so-called "World Championship Events" holds about thirty world ranked tournaments a year with over 200 divisions! That means that they possibly crown over 6,000 so-called "World Champions" each year! Can you say…SCAM!

At this point, you may be wondering why any of this matters. If parents and unsuspecting students are happy with the instruction they are getting from these McDojos, then what's the problem. Well, one of the problems is when the students actually believe they are getting real martial arts training and can truly defend themselves with the training they have received.

When these instructors build up a student's confidence in his false abilities, it puts the student in a dangerous position. This is especially true if the student ever tries to use his "skills" in a real life-or-death situation. Sparring is a game, with rules and protection; fighting for your life against a seasoned, dangerous predator, intent on harming you, is something completely different.

If a student who has only trained for tournaments and sparring believes that he is prepared to take on a savvy street fighter, he is badly mistaken. His false confidence could get him badly hurt or even killed.

Another issue with these McDojos, and the questionable instructors who run them, is one which those outside of the martial arts world almost never consider. If the instructor is a fraud, then the rank that he is giving to his students is actually not valid. This means that his students are actually being defrauded.

I have seen fraudulent instructors, who cross-promoted themselves from 4th or 5th degree black belts to 10th degree grandmasters, actually promoting students to the rank of 7th and 8th degree black belt. They did not have the authority to promote anyone to these high ranks because they do not even hold those ranks themselves.

These unsuspecting students have no idea that their costly promotion is not worth the paper it was printed on! This is no different than some sleazy conman conning someone out of their money. The catch is, it can be hard to prove, so most of these guys get away with it. Later, these students may promote their own students to advance rank, and the cycle continues.

These kinds of instructors are called paper tigers. They don't truly have the rank which they profess to have; they merely have a piece of paper which states that they have that rank. They didn't earn it; they maneuvered, manipulated, and schemed their way to getting a piece of paper which states that they have the rank, but that is all.

Thus, the term "paper tigers." Their rank only exists on a worthless piece of paper.

There is a "martial artist" in California who many in the martial arts world know, who claims that Frank Dux, whose life story was portrayed in the movie "Blood Sport," promoted him to 10th degree black belt and gave him the title of grandmaster. Knowing Frank personally, I called him and asked him if that was true. Frank said that he never promoted this hack to any rank and that he had never given anyone the title of grandmaster.

This is a perfect example of how these fraudulent instructors con potential students and parents. He has a fraudulent certificate which he probably bought himself. He promoted himself to 10th degree black belt and stuck Frank Dux's name on the certificate, knowing that 99% of his potential students and parents would not have a way to contact Frank and fact check his lie. And even if they did, almost all of them would simply take his word for it.

Then he used his fake rank to promote his McDojo, which has since gone under (thank God!), and to market himself as a student of Frank Dux, a well-known martial arts master. The student off the street sees Hanshi Dux's name on the certificate and thinks he is going to get some top quality instruction from this instructor, when in fact, it is all a big con job.

Unethical instructors and outright fakes abound in the martial arts, and they are only interested in self-promotion and money. If you are looking for good martial arts classes, always keep in mind that anyone can claim to be a martial arts master or grandmaster, open a dojo in some strip mall, and start teaching classes.

Every year, more and more people sign up for martial arts instruction for self-defense and are finding that they are no more able to defend themselves in a real life self-defense situation than they were before they started training. These McDojos give students a false sense of confidence, but do not give them the techniques or skills to go along with their newly found self-confidence. Again, you simply must do your homework!

31

You must understand, while these dojos may offer a fun workout, so does Zumba or spinning classes. If you are trying to learn true martial arts or self-defense from an instructor who does not have the real experience to back it up, you are wasting your money. Buyer beware!

Real self-defense and true martial arts are nothing like what you will find in these McDojos, although the McDojo instructors will never tell you this. These dojos are all smoke and mirrors! They may look the same to the untrained eye, but they are as different as night and day.

McDojos are mainly focused on sports martial arts because that is the best way for them to market themselves, and because these instructors actually know very little about true martial arts. They get some flashy uniforms made, which serves as advertising for the dojo. They train almost entirely for competition, as the instructor has little to no experience in self-defense or in the deeper aspects of the arts. And they mainly market themselves to parents of young children, usually with a large turnover from year to year.

I have given you several warning signs that a dojo might be a McDojo with questionable instructors and practices, but I want to end this chapter by giving a list of warning signs to look for when considering a martial arts dojo for yourself or your child.

The 30 Warning Signs of a McDojo

1) High pressure to get students/parents to sign a long term contract

2) The instructor claims an extremely high belt rank at a young age

3) Classes are very expensive

4) Claims about their art being thousands of years old or the best in the world

5) Claims to be a former Special Forces guy or have a Special Forces guy on the staff

6) Pre-adolescent children with black belts

7) Guarantees that you will receive a black belt in a certain amount of time

8) Claims that the art being taught is the instructor's *personal variation* of the art

9) Excessively frequent belt tests or promotions

10) Claims that their system can train you to be a deadly martial artist in a short period of time

11) The instructor is under 40-50 years old and claims to be a 9th or 10th degree black belt

12) Lack of sparring in a contact heavy art

13) Multi-colored, silly looking gis

14) Teaches the techniques but not the applications

15) Advertises non-contact martial arts

16) You see uniforms with tons of patches everywhere

17) Rank advancement is very expensive

18) Extra-wide, fancy belts

19) Ranks higher than 10th degree black belt

20) Trophies all over the dojo

21) Spends excessive time on katas or forms

22) Doing katas to music

23) Nobody ever fails the belt tests

24) Kids classes are mostly games and chaos instead of actual martial arts instruction

25) Rank advancement is time based rather than achievement based

26) Instructors rarely teach philosophy, strategy, or applications

27) Kiais are nothing more than super loud screaming

28) No touch knockout claims

29) Your instructor requires students to call him grandmaster or master outside of class

30) You see a lot of backflips and gymnastics

While there are many more warning signs, these should give you a good idea of what to look for to avoid these McDojos. McDojos are not only unethical as they con students and parents out of a lot of money, but they also can give students a dangerous sense of over-confidence, as I stated earlier. Most instructors in these McDojos have never been in a real fight in their lives, which means they can't prepare anyone else for these situations either.

I also want to point out that just because you see some of these warning signs in a dojo, that is not an absolute sign that the dojo is a McDojo. For example, if the dojo is totally focused on sports martial arts, it would be expected that they would be proud of their trophies which their students have won and may have a trophy case or trophies in the dojo.

Also, many sports oriented martial arts dojos do have uniforms which are non-traditional and represent their dojo. While these uniforms may not be the traditional white gis, that does not automatically mean that the instructor is not qualified or that his dojo is a McDojo.

Moreover, many dojos have retired Special Forces guys who teach martial arts for a living. But most of the time, these guys do not go around bragging about their experiences. In fact, the martial artists I have known who are retired Special Forces guys, don't like talking about their military experiences. Most have done things and had experiences which they don't talk about, even to their closest friends, and they sure don't brag about them.

If a martial arts instructor starts bragging about how many people he killed in Iraq or Vietnam, you can be fairly sure that he is a fraud. I have never known a legitimate Special Forces guy who liked to brag or even discuss much of what he did in the military in that way. That should be a giant red flag for you!

The 30 Warning Signs of a McDojo is simply a rough guide; it is not a set of hard and fast rules. But if you find that a dojo which you are considering exhibits several of these warning signs, you may want to do more research on them and think twice before signing up to train with them, especially if you are serious about your martial arts training.

If you are only interested in a fun hobby or sport, it may not be that big of a deal, but if you are serious about learning self-defense, you will want to make sure that what you are being taught actually works and that your instructor knows what he is talking about.

McDojos are nothing more than moneymaking machines. Most legitimate martial arts masters teach for the love of their art, not because they think they can make a killing teaching martial arts. Most of the best instructors I have trained with have taught classes in their garages, their back yard, or in the park.

When it comes to serious martial arts classes, it is the instruction, the knowledge, the skills, and teaching abilities of the instructor that matters, not some fancy looking dojo. Don't be wowed by photos of an instructor with martial arts celebrities or movie stars. Anyone can go to martial arts events and get photos taken with martial arts celebrities; those photos are meaningless as far as your training goes. Focus on substance, not appearances!

In the next chapter, I will touch on what my friend, Sifu Al Dacascos, calls the grandmaster pandemic, fraudulent martial arts masters, paper tigers, and more. The dark side of the martial arts is about to get even darker!

I refuse to lower my standards to
accommodate those who refuse to raise theirs.
Steve Gamlin

Chapter 4
Fraudulent Masters and Grandmasters

Things do not pass for what they are, but for what they seem…
things are judged by how they look, even though most
things are far different from what they appear.
Baltasar Gracian

The number of fraudulent masters and grandmasters in the martial arts community has reached the level of a pandemic. When I started martial arts back in 1984, I never heard the term "grandmaster" in the Japanese martial arts. Now, it seems everywhere you look, there is another martial artist claiming to be a grandmaster, and it seems that almost everyone is claiming to be a martial arts master. I have even seen kids who claim to be martial arts masters!

Consider this, in the Korean martial arts, they use the English terms of "Master" and "Grandmaster" based on education and training level. In Korea, you can get a university degree in martial arts or attend master and grandmaster level courses. The truth is, even today, only about twenty non-Koreans have ever graduated from those courses.

I discuss these and more martial arts titles in detail in the next chapter, so I won't get into what they mean here. This chapter is more about the pandemic of martial arts frauds in the martial arts community who claim to be masters and grandmasters.

I quickly touched on the term "paper tigers" in the last chapter. Paper tiger is the term used for martial artists who have the ranks, titles, etc., but through certificates only. Basically, they have the certificates, but not the training, thus, the term "paper" tiger. They have somehow bought, traded, or maneuvered to get a certificate which declares them to be a master or grandmaster, or even made their own certificate, but they never did the training or actually *earned* their rank or title.

In the old days of the martial arts, to get a black belt certificate or a certificate for advanced rank, you had to get them from a legitimate instructor. There was no internet, no personal computers or fancy printers. To get certificates printed up, you had to go through an actual printer, and you had to pay for quite a few at a time. You couldn't simply go in and order one certificate, or if you did, the cost would be very expensive. Certificates were simply not easy to come by.

Now, you can find martial arts certificates for sale all over the internet. In addition, most people have computers and printers, and have the ability to make their own certificates and print them themselves. We also have print shops where you can get copies made very cheaply.

This advancement in technology has made it much easier and/or cheaper for fraudulent martial arts masters to buy or print their own fake certificates and use them to con unsuspecting students and parents. Of course, these fake certificates are totally worthless, but the uninitiated students and parents do not know that. They simply see the fancy certificate on the wall and take it at face value.

Furthermore, with the use of scanners and photo editing software, martial arts frauds are able to take a legitimate certificate, scan it, and Photoshop it with their name on it. Con artists have always been very skilled at making themselves appear legitimate when they aren't; that is what con artists do. And the martial arts world is packed full of these con artists called paper tigers.

In fact, there is a fraudulent martial arts master from Missoula, MT (who I won't name as I refuse to give these frauds free publicity) who wrote a book on exactly how to fake your martial arts credentials. He included things which only a fraud like himself would know how to do or would even consider doing. You don't get any lower than that in the martial arts world! It is one thing to be a fraud, and another to actually teach people how to defraud others. Only a true con artist or criminal would do such a thing. Disgusting!

Using his own experience in faking his own fraudulent credentials, he guides unscrupulous martial artists on how to fake their credentials, fake photographs, fake certificates, what to do and what not to do, etc. His book, along with his life, are a total disgrace! Yet, he still has students where he teaches sham classes at some gym a couple of nights a week. This is a perfect example of a fraudulent martial arts master. Absolutely pathetic!

And when anyone questions this fraud about his credentials, he whips out fake certificates, fake letters, fake photographs, etc. to prove that he is legitimate. The most ridiculous thing is that most people simply accept these fake documents as reality when they are anything but. He has even made fraudulent claims about being a sniper and a sniper instructor, which used to be called stolen valor and was punishable by law, but President Obama changed the stolen valor laws, so he is able to get away with his false claims.

While this guy may sound like the exception to the rule, I assure you that there are more of these fake martial arts masters in the martial arts world than you realize. I have run across these kinds of frauds from Seattle to New York and everywhere in between. Where there is money to be made, you will find these con artists and fraudulent masters doing their best to fleece another student or parent out of their hard-earned money.

There are no lengths that these fraudulent martial arts masters won't go to in order to make a name, and another dollar, for themselves. I know of a fraudulent "grandmaster" in Seattle who is a self-proclaimed "living legend." He is a complete fraud, but markets himself as a grandmaster, a living legend, and a martial arts hall of fame inductee. (I will cover the martial arts hall of fame frauds in another chapter.)

This guy has tried every trick in the book to try and make a name for himself. He has a student, a graphic design artist, who makes bogus certificates for him so he can market his own bogus martial arts federation. He has had him make nice looking book covers for books which have never existed and, by the writing skills which he exhibits on social media, never will.

He carries a fake badge and claims to have worked for the Sheriff's department, which he never worked for. At one time, he was advertising that he had a program to get your black belt in less than a year. He was marketing a program where he comes into your home and trains you in your house. I am not sure he still markets that after a lady claimed she paid him $35 for a private lesson, and he sexually assaulted her in 2017.

This guy even offered to "knight" a friend of mine and claimed that he comes from a royal family and has the ability to knight people. While this sounds too crazy to believe, it is all true! He told my friend that he was going to have her kneel at his feet, take his sword, and actually make her a knight! I guess reality really *is* stranger than fiction!

He is constantly trying any gimmick and any con to help him get some kind of foothold in the martial arts world. And the scary thing is that he is not even close to being the only nut job/conman in the martial arts world today. You can run across these fraudulent martial arts masters all over the country. It truly is a shame that they con so many people out of money and rob people of the true martial arts training which people really want and truly deserve from a martial arts master.

And the real shame is that most people in the martial arts world actually know that this guy is a total fraud and that he is mentally unbalanced, but no one really seems to care. He is a joke to those who know him, but many still allow him to come to their martial arts events and give sham seminars and talks.

As I stated, these frauds will go to great lengths to try to "prove" that they are legitimate. They make up fraudulent documents, fake photographs, con other martial artists into believing in them and then use those martial artists' names to try to legitimize themselves. They even take their belts and rip them to shreds to show that they have been training for so long that their belts are wearing out. All of this is abhorrent to legitimate martial artists, but most simply turn a blind eye to these despicable actions.

It has gotten so bad that now you can even buy your black belt with different degrees of wear and tear on it. You can get it 25%, 50%,

70%, or 90% worn out; all you have to do is pay for it. These are called pre-worn out black belts or "vintage" black belts. If this is not fraudulent, I don't know what is! The advertisement below is an example of a company selling these "vintage" black belts. Notice how the fancy kanji and names on these belts are never worn out, just the rest of the belt.

Others simply choose to falsely wear out the belt themselves by scraping it on rough concrete, dragging it behind their car, running a belt sander on it, or washing it excessively, etc. All to give other martial artists and students the impression that they wore their black belt out through daily training over years and years. It is a total scam!

The photo on the next page shows a "martial artist" wearing a belt which has obviously been purposely worn out on all parts besides his name. I guess when you are trying to convince people that you are a legitimate grandmaster, they have to be able to read your name on the belt. Notice how there is no wear on the part of the belt where his name is embroidered, but the rest of the belt is almost completely worn out.

When you purposely wear out your black belt, but still want your name to show clearly.

I have also seen black belts which are nothing more than torn shreds of cotton. Since your black belt should not be washed and should be kept nicely folded when not being worn, just think how many years it would take for a belt to get that torn up with normal use and proper care.

It would take an incredible number of years to completely wear out a nice, heavy black belt to the point that it is pretty much completely white. And that is exactly why these fraudulent masters purposely wear out their belts. They are desperately trying to convince everyone that they have trained so hard, for so long, that they even wore their black belt out.

Another telltale sign of a fake martial arts master is young guys claiming to be a martial arts master or grandmaster. By definition, a master is someone who has acquired complete knowledge or skill in their art. If you are a master of your trade, whether it is being a plumber, an electrician, or a martial artist, it means that you have completely mastered that art.

Does anyone truly think that someone in their 20's or 30's has acquired complete mastery of the martial arts? Is it even possible for someone that age to have mastered not only the skills necessary for complete mastery, but the mental maturity, the wisdom, and the spiritual insight that a true martial arts master should have?

A grandmaster should not only have all of those qualities, but many more. He should also have great wisdom gained from decades of martial arts and living life in general. In addition, he should have a certain amount of advanced black belts under him. I am not going to get into all the knowledge and skills a true grandmaster should have in this chapter.

My friend and mentor, Sifu Al Dacascos actually wrote an amazing, in depth chapter on what it means to be a grandmaster in my book series, *Secrets of the Martial Arts Masters*. If you are interested in what a real martial arts master or grandmaster should be, I encourage you to pick up a copy of that two-volume set, as there are several chapters on the topic.

But for this discussion, it is enough to point out that it would be extremely rare for any young man or woman to truly have all the qualifications, physically, mentally, and spiritually to truly be a real martial arts master, much less a grandmaster. And yet, you can see young martial artists all across the country who claim to be martial arts masters and some who claim to be grandmasters.

As a consumer you may feel that you can do a simple internet search to find a real master. The problem is that the internet is like the Wild West in that the fake masters go out of their way to write lies and even make fake business reviews to destroy the reputation of good martial arts instructors in their area. Several of the highest-ranking martial artists that I know have been the victims of these fake reviews and have been dealing with this slanderous and libelous activity for years.

Again, the advancement in technology is being used in a fraudulent way by these dishonest martial artists. In the past, you had to have a computer expert make a website for you; and even then, that website was not customizable like blogs are today. Today, anyone can make their own website or blog in just a few hours, and they can then write anything they want on that blog or site. They can trash other martial artists, calling them fakes and frauds, and they can write fraudulent information about themselves under fake names to make themselves look legitimate.

This makes it extremely hard to distinguish between true martial arts masters and grandmasters and the fakes and frauds who have simply acquired their title and rank fraudulently. This is one reason we are now seeing so many martial arts masters and grandmasters today. The internet is absolutely *not* a reliable source of information when it comes to verifying a martial artist's rank or title! I have learned to believe very little of what I read on the internet, at least until I have verified it through several trustworthy sources.

The lack of morals, honor and integrity has led to this pandemic of fake masters and grandmasters. When martial arts masters and grandmasters are willing to lower their standards and give their friends and acquaintances rank and titles which they have not earned, it causes a lot of confusion, hard feelings, and distrust within the martial arts community. These fraudulent activities are so common that the vast majority of martial artists don't know what to do about it or how to slow it down, much less put a stop to it.

In the next chapter, I will look at the obsession with martial arts titles a little closer and discuss the meaning of these titles and why so many fraudulent "martial artists" use these fancy sounding titles and how they actually "acquire" them.

The warrior is not led by others;
but by remaining true to his convictions.
F. J. Chu

44

Chapter 5
Title Obsession

Having the idea is not living the reality.
Rumi

Martial arts is supposed to be about respect, humility, self-defense, and improving yourself – spirit, mind, and body. But in modern times, the use of titles such as master, grandmaster, senior grandmaster, supreme grandmaster, supreme chief grandmaster, etc. have become a pandemic in the martial arts world. Where did these titles come from and what meaning do they really carry?

Toshiro Mifune achieved more worldwide fame than any other Japanese actor of his century. Toshiro Mifune became known to most Americans for his role in the movie Red Sun co-starring with Charles Bronson. In his later years he gained new fame in the title role of the American TV miniseries Shogun (1980) and appeared infrequently in cameo roles after that. In 1983, at a dinner of NHK television executives, he gave this explanation of the use of the titles "Master" and "Grandmaster" in the martial arts movie genre.

Toshiro Mifune stated that, in the arts of Kung Fu and Karate, many of these titles were created by British translators who were doing voice over work in the 1960's and 1970's for a new genre of movies called "Chop Socky" movies. These were low budget martial arts movies coming out of Hong Kong and China that started gaining a worldwide cult following. People who watched these movies and wanted to learn how to do the moves that they saw in movies such as *Five Fingers of Death* and *The Flying Guillotine* started seeking a "Master" to teach them. Thus, the "Master of Karate" was born.

An instructor from a school in Savannah, Georgia once stated that someone visited his class and asked, "Are you a master?" He laughed and said no because he thought it was a silly question. Then the person walked out. This happened a few more times, and he realized that these people didn't understand the titles, so they left thinking that they needed to find a "Master" to study with. After that, he started using the title of "Master" to make these prospective students more comfortable.

Most potential students and parents have no idea about the meanings of the different martial arts titles. To them, they sound foreign, intriguing, and maybe a bit mysterious and mystical. Fraudulent martial arts "masters" understand this all too well. Therefore, they take advantage of this fact and use these titles to impress potential students and parents concerning their expertise in the martial arts. When all a new student knows about martial arts comes from television or movies, it is easy for these dishonest martial artists to use the new student's ignorance to their advantage.

A martial arts title is supposed to designate what authority you hold in that particular organization or style of martial art; whereas, your rank represents your progress in your martial art. It seems, especially in the West, that martial artists have become obsessed with self-important titles which serve little purpose other than to stroke each other's egos. Although the titles may vary from style to style, the most common terms are consistent.

Here is a list of some of the more common traditional martial arts titles and what they mean:

Japanese Titles

Kohai – Junior Student
Senpai – Senior Student
Sensei – Teacher
Renshi – Polished Teacher
Kyoshi – Expert Teacher
Shihan – Expert
Soke – Head of Family
Hanshi – Teacher of Teachers

Korean Titles

GupJa – Color Belt Student
YuDanJa – Black Belt Student

Hu Bae Nim – Junior Student
Sun Bae Nim – Senior Student
Sah Bum Nim – Instructor
Sah Boo Nim – Teaching Father
Chung Sah Nim – Chief Instructor
Kwan Jang Nim – Head of Organization
Chong Kwan Jang Nim – Head of Style

Chinese Titles

Sifu – Teaching Father
Sigung – Sifu's Teacher
Zongshi - Founder

According to Grandmaster Richard Hackworth, "In Korea, being a martial arts teacher is a legitimate profession, and you can earn a university degree in it. The titles of Sah Bum Nim and Sah Boo Nim fall under the 'Master' of the art group for advanced training courses. While Chung Sah Nim, Kwan Jang Nim, and Chong Kwan Jan Nim fall under the Grandmasters courses. Meaning that, in Korean martial arts, you must take those courses to have earned those titles.

Being a master of the art allows you to teach professionally without anyone senior to you supervising your class. Being a 'Grandmaster' of the craft or art, designates you as someone who has the authority and skills to mentor those who follow you on that career path training as new masters. It is very similar to the title of Professor at a university, nothing more."

Let's get real. These titles mean no more than the meanings which their translations confer. They are simply words in the original language which carry a specific meaning. While there is absolutely nothing wrong with using these titles, especially in a martial arts setting, they are not mystical and do not carry any mysterious power or meaning. They are simply Asian words, period. Calling someone "sensei" is no different than calling someone "teacher." Calling someone a Hanshi simply means that they are a teacher of teachers, nothing more.

47

Also, if you will notice, there are no titles which translate to master or grandmaster. The title of master simply signifies someone who has mastered his art, whether it is the art of sword making or being a plumber. The title of grandmaster is simply a Western bastardization which has arisen from the egotistical nature of many martial artists and has nothing to do with most traditional martial arts, other than what I just covered from Korea. Although it has become an acceptable term for an elderly martial arts master.

Martial arts titles originally paralleled the family relationship where the older, more experienced father or grandfather was revered. They were not used as some form of award or to make them feel good about themselves. They never demanded to be called by their title, but rather, it was a way of the younger family members or students to show honor and respect to their elders.

Too many martial artists today use these titles to indulge their own egos. Many simply award themselves these titles; they don't come from a recognized governing body or a legitimate elder martial artist. They haven't earned them with decades of work to perfect their art, and they haven't been awarded these titles because of the respect or honor they have gained from teaching hundreds of students. They just decide to anoint themselves, trade favors for their titles, or simply buy them.

Some titles come with specific martial arts rank and others can simply be awarded to someone as an honorary title. Both of these are acceptable ways of being awarded a martial arts title; giving yourself the title or "trading favors" for your title or rank is never acceptable, but has become common place in today's martial arts world.

There is an old Japanese maxim which states, "You become a shihan when another shihan starts referring to you as such." If you were not awarded a specific title by a respected martial artist who has earned both respect and his title, your title is bogus, period.

The Western martial arts community has become obsessed with the superficial aspects of the martial arts instead of focusing on their actual martial arts skills. Martial arts is supposed to be about self-improvement, not self-promotion. But many martial artists are more concerned with titles, rank, and superficial appearances than they are in improving their martial arts skills, their character, their mind, and their spirit. And there lies the problem!

Let's delve into the subject of using titles such as grandmaster, senior grandmaster, and supreme grandmaster a little deeper. Here is an interesting fact. No other community uses these types of grandiose titles outside of the martial arts community.

While there are master plumbers, master electricians, master carpenters, you have never heard of a grandmaster electrician, a grandmaster plumber, or a grandmaster carpenter. Why is that? The answer is really simple – you are either a master of your art or you are not.

If you are a master swordsmith, you are a master at that trade. Being a master of your trade means that you have mastered all aspects of that art. That doesn't mean that you have reached the point where you cannot make improvements in your skills, but it does mean that you have become proficient at your chosen art and made it your own. Likewise, if you have mastered the art of self-defense or have mastered your style of martial art, you are a martial arts master.

Being a master of your art has traditionally been enough for martial artists. But in modern times, it appears that mastering your art is not enough for many martial artists. The out-of-control egos of many martial artists must have some way to show they are better than the average master; so they came up with a greater title to set themselves apart – grandmaster.

I find it humorous that being a master was good enough for Gichin Funakoshi, Miyamoto Musashi, and other traditional martial arts masters, but it is somehow lacking or not good enough for today's modern martial artists. If you have actually mastered your art, can you truly be greater than that or are these additional titles nothing more than people's egos running amuck? What has happened to humility in the martial arts world?

We only see this arrogance and self-importance in the martial arts community, as I pointed out. I defy anyone to show me a master plumber who calls himself a grandmaster plumber or a supreme grandmaster plumber. They are either a master in their chosen field or they are not. So why do we see so many martial artists who are not satisfied being a master of their art? The answer lies in one word – EGO. They are constantly trying to show that they are better than someone else.

Once you get acquainted with a lot of people in the martial arts world, it doesn't take long to recognize that a lot of martial artists have issues with overblown egos. Many got into the martial arts to start with because they were bullied, assaulted, or harassed for years. And even after they have mastered many martial arts skills and techniques, they still carry that chip on their shoulder. They are determined never to be bullied or assaulted again, and understandably so.

When they started martial arts, many had self-esteem issues because of the bullying, assault, or years of harassment. Martial arts is a great way to help rebuild someone's self-confidence and self-esteem and has worked miracles for many people. This is one of the wonderful things about the martial arts.

Martial arts is meant to help people live a better life, not simply to learn how to fight or to be an entertaining and fun hobby or sport. As Miyamoto Musashi stated, "The true science of martial arts means practicing them in such a way that they will be useful at any time, and to teach them in such a way that they will be useful in all things."

On the other hand, some people go from one extreme to the other. They go from very low self-esteem to an overblown sense of self-importance. That chip on their shoulder morphs into a giant ego as they accomplish more and more in the martial arts world. With that giant ego comes the need for more recognition to set them apart from the rest of the crowd, thus the need for higher and more grandiose titles. No longer does it suffice to be a martial arts master. They need to be called grandmaster. And with more and more people becoming grandmasters, the title "grandmaster" has become so common place that it has almost lost its meaning.

So what do these martial artists do to address this egotistical challenge? They come up with a higher title – senior grandmaster, supreme grandmaster, or supreme chief grandmaster. One hack even calls himself the "Godfather of the Martial Arts." Talk about ego!

As more and more people start to use these increasingly more narcissistic titles, I am sure we will see newer, higher titles appear in the martial arts world. These people seem to always be looking for another way to set themselves apart from the herd.

These ostentatious titles have become a joke to many true martial artists. While there is nothing wrong with the traditional titles, as long as they are earned by honest means or given by legitimate martial artists, there can be no doubt that many traditional titles are being misused for purely egotistical purposes today.

Furthermore, the new titles such as supreme grandmaster, supreme chief grandmaster, senior grandmaster, etc. are simply meaningless egotistical titles altogether. You won't find any of these martial arts titles in traditional martial arts. They are a modern invention.

When I first met Sifu Al Dacascos, we had many deep, philosophical conversations. Before I got to know Sifu Al, I called him Grandmaster Dacascos. Sifu Al quickly corrected me saying, "Bohdi, don't call me grandmaster or master. Just call me Sifu or Al. There is only one master and that is Jesus."

Now, everyone who keeps up with martial arts knows who Sifu Al Dacascos is. He has been on dozens and dozens of magazine covers and is a true martial artist in every way. He was one of the top fighters during his competitive years, competing with everyone from Mike Stone to Chuck Norris. He was also a personal friend of Bruce Lee and the Lee family, and was offered the part of Bruce Lee in a movie about Bruce Lee. Linda Lee also offered Sifu Al all of Bruce's clothes and gear after his death, but Sifu Al politely declined the offer.

Sifu Al has stayed with me at my home, and we have spent many hours training together. Even in his 70's, Sifu Al is the best martial artist I have ever trained with. His speed, quickness, skills, and martial arts knowledge are unsurpassed. He is absolutely a master of his art.

Yet, with all of his credentials and experience, he always corrects anyone who calls him "master" or "grandmaster." He is absolutely, hands down, the best, most skilled martial artist I have ever worked with, and yet he refuses to be called a master. This is the humble attitude of a true martial artist and a true martial arts master!

Has Sifu Al mastered the art of self-defense? Absolutely! Has he mastered the art of Kajukenbo? Yes, of course. He has even developed his own style of martial art, Wun Hop Kuen Do, with schools throughout the world. And yet, he refuses to be called a master or grandmaster out of a sense of humility and respect for his beliefs and the martial arts. THAT, in my book, is the character of a true martial arts grandmaster.

Compare that with some of the so-called grandmasters of today who give themselves the title of grandmaster and *demand* that others call them grandmaster so-and-so whenever they are in public.

Sifu Al Dacascos is humble, real, respectful, loyal, down to earth, and one of the greatest martial arts teachers of his time. Whereas, some of these so-called "grandmasters," "supreme grandmasters," and self-proclaimed "living legends" are arrogant, demanding, disloyal, conceited, and are as fraudulent as a three dollar bill. Are you starting to see the distinctions?

No one questions how Sifu Al Dacascos earned his respect or his title of grandmaster, even though he is too humble to use it – he earned it through years of hard work and dedication, his skills, and what he has given back to the martial arts. And, in my humble opinion, he absolutely deserves it.

Deserving a title such as "Grandmaster" does not come from mastering your art, that is what the title "Master" signifies. Being a grandmaster comes from the respect you have achieved for what you have *given back* to the martial arts community.

If you are giving nothing back, I don't care how great your skills are, you absolutely do not deserve the title of grandmaster. Sifu Al is a great example of someone who has given back to the martial arts community for most of his life and continues to share his teachings and knowledge with those who want to learn, even throughout his golden years.

In contrast, there are many others in the martial arts world who went about getting their titles by different means. Sifu Al's traditional training is in Kajukenbo, where he earned his rank, title, and skills through hard work and training. I also know other martial artists who use the title of Grandmaster in Kajukenbo, who have never practiced Kajukenbo at all. They never even earned a 1st degree black belt in Kajukenbo. This is a disgrace!

They did not earn their titles. These are not honorary titles given to them for their contributions to the martial arts community. So how did they become Kajukenbo grandmasters? Well, the short answer is – THEY AREN'T! But since that doesn't actually answer the question of how they obtained their titles, I will delve a little deeper into this topic.

There are many ways that unscrupulous martial artists obtain titles which they did not earn and which were not awarded to them by legitimate martial arts masters. And none of these ways are on the up and up, but it seems that the majority of martial artists turn a blind eye to these underhanded practices.

One of the ways that these dishonest martial artists obtain the title of grandmaster is to become a "founder" of their own style of martial art. Essentially, they "develop" their "new" style of martial art and then, as the "founder," award themselves with a 10th degree black belt and the title of grandmaster.

Basically, they take existing techniques, forms, katas, etc., tweak them in some small way, make up some new name, and declare that they have founded a new martial arts style or system. Since it is a "new" style, and they "developed" it, they consider it proper that they be called a grandmaster of "MeSo Great Do."

Many then start a federation or organization and begin to sign up new members of their "new" art, giving those new members rank under them as the grandmaster of "MeSo Great Do." This is done to legitimize the new art and to build a following. This is a little like a Ponzi scheme or a martial art multi-level marketing scheme where the guys who get in on the ground floor get high ranks and titles and then market the new product (the new art) to other martial artists who join the band wagon.

Can anyone start a new martial arts style and award himself a 10th degree black belt and the title of grandmaster? Actually, yes. There is no law against it. Technically it is not illegal, but it is definitely immoral, unethical, and dishonest; that is, unless you have developed a style of self-defense that is totally different from anything out there or which makes an existing style much more functional. And, once again, since there is no governing body in the martial arts community, martial artists get away with doing this over and over again. But doing this does not make them a legitimate grandmaster.

Xiao Ma, Sales Director for World Martial Arts Media and a 2nd degree black belt in the Korean self-defense art of Hapkido and a 1st degree black belt in traditional Taekwondo, interviewed Grandmaster Yong Hon Kim, President of the Korean TangSooDo MuDukKwan Society, about the two ways in which one can become a founder of a new martial arts. Here is an excerpt of that interview.

"Xiao Ma: Hello Sir. Thank you for agreeing to this interview. It is a great privilege to meet with you today.

Yong Hon Kim: It is an honor to do this for World Martial Arts Magazine. This is sure to help the martial arts community in many ways by dispelling the myths that surround the martial arts culture.

Xiao Ma: The first topic on my list is, how does someone become the founder of a martial art?

Yong Hon Kim: That is a great question because there is a lot of confusion in the martial arts community about how this is done and the answer is very simple. There are only two ways for someone to legitimately be recognized as the founder of a traditional martial art.

The first way is to come up with a unique way to apply the principles of martial arts to standard scenarios that is different from other recognized systems. The quality of the system will determine if and when the martial arts community would recognize the system as a new and _unique_ martial art. Once the system has been established and at least ten schools are teaching this system, then the founder can apply for recognition from an authoritative body such as the Korean Martial Arts Instructors Association, the World Grand Masters Council of Martial Arts, or the World Martial Arts Congress.

To apply, the founder would submit a written curriculum for review to show that his system covers all of the federation requirements for each rank. Once this curriculum has been matched to the standards, the founder would do a presentation for the board of directors for evaluation. This presentation would show how the system applies their _unique_ method to the training scenarios within the curriculum. If a majority of the reviewing committee agrees that this system is _unique_ in its application, then a Letter of Style Recognition will be granted to the founder.

Xiao Ma: That is very interesting. I have heard some of that before but it seems very systematic and free of politics.

Yong Hon Kim: Standards are the opposite of politics. Politics are when an instructor uses his influence or money to buy off an official for the paperwork that they don't qualify for. I have seen a lot of this in the last few years. It lowers the quality of teaching and it has ruined the arts in the last twenty years. Things aren't the same now.

Xiao Ma: I agree with you completely Sir. Please tell us more about how someone becomes recognized as a founder of a martial art.

Yong Hon Kim: Of course. Well the second way that someone becomes recognized as a style founder is through the scientific method of establishment. Every generation of grandmasters will meet on occasion to discuss problems of applications found within the system. They state the problems and then gather information on what is observed during the occurrence of the problem.

After the problems have been clearly identified and documented the grandmasters form a hypothesis of what would correct the problem. They would then hold clinics testing the hypothesis with other masters and grandmasters as witnesses of the testing. They would then analyze the data and develop changes and adjustments to what is practiced based on the conclusions of the analysis. This new information is presented to the governing body and once reviewed can be approved. The head grandmaster is designated as the founder of a new style name that is recognized as the next generation of that art.

For example, Choi Young Sool practiced Hapkido YuSool, which is just the Korean translation for the martial art that he learned in Japan. He is the founder. Those students of his who began kwans based on his teaching, but with their new adjustments, became founders of their style or kwan.

Those are the only two recognized ways to because a founder and it must be under the approval of the recognized organizations that I mentioned earlier."

What Grandmaster Yong Hon Kim described here is far different than what many so-called "grandmasters" are getting away with today. I know a couple of guys who started a bogus martial arts federation (I won't give the name of the federation, as I don't want to give them any publicity), and then cross-promoted each other to the rank of 10th degree black belt and the titles of Hanshi.

These two used their bogus federation and promptly bought ridiculous looking "grandmaster" belts to go along with their new self-promoted titles of "grandmaster." One of the belts was so wide that he couldn't even tie his belt properly. After posting photos of himself with his ridiculous looking belt, people started making derogatory comments about it. He quickly bought a different belt to try to put a stop to all the questions about his legitimacy.

Nothing changed in their martial arts skills or background, except for a bogus certificate in which they cross-promoted each other to their new ranks and title. One went from 5th dan to 10th overnight and the other from 7th dan to 10th overnight.

They did not develop a new style and did not have anything unique; they simply decided to start a new federation and awarded each other a new, higher rank. Their actions were not sanctioned by any governing body; it was just a sham. But none of that stopped them from getting their new rank or titles.

A little while after they awarded each other 10th dans, they started awarding other students higher ranks, such as 7th dan and 8th dan. This is another great example of paper tiger frauds and how they scam unsuspecting martial artists. Little did their students know that neither of these two clowns had the authority to promote them to these advanced ranks. It truly is shameful.

Many bogus martial arts masters pull this little sleight of hand trick. They simply start a new martial arts federation or organization, award each other 10th degree black belts and the titles of grandmaster, and then start recruiting new martial artists under their organization or federation in an attempt to legitimize their rank and title.

Many of these people practice Korean arts. Keep in mind that there is *no* 10th degree black belt rank in Korean martial arts. This proves their ignorance about their own style of martial art, and it also proves that they are not even a master of their art, much less a grandmaster. The only thing these people are masters of is conning other martial artists through the use of technology and dishonest means. Anyone using the rank of 10th degree black belt in Korean martial arts should be avoided at all costs!

Compare these clowns in this example with what I shared about a true grandmaster, Sifu Al Dacascos. It is not like comparing apples and oranges; it is more like comparing apples with rotten tomatoes. It is simply a scam to get an undeserved rank and titles for people who feel entitled and want a shortcut to their martial arts goals, instead of putting in the time and effort to actually *earn* their rank and titles. This practice should be offensive to every legitimate martial artist!

This leads me to the question of why do these guys do this? They have to know deep inside their spirit that getting a piece of paper with a bogus rank or title on it, doesn't change who they truly are, or their true rank. Is this just a matter of out-of-control egos or is there something darker and more sinister going on here?

Actually, in my opinion, it is both. As I have already discussed, there are a lot of people in the martial arts with huge egos. They feel they are just as good as those with higher ranks or titles; so they simply find a way to get the rank and title that they *feel* they deserve. If they can't get promoted traditionally, they sell their honor and get what they desire in less honorable ways.

But this is only one side of the coin. The other side of the coin goes back to the root of all evil – the love of money. If there is a dojo on the other side of town run by Grandmaster Lee, and John Boy is running his dojo but only has the rank of 4th dan, it might be hard for John Boy to compete. So what does he do?

Well, he figures out a way to make himself equal to Grandmaster Lee. He schemes to start a new federation with his best buddy, and they each promote each other to 10th dan and the title of grandmaster. Now John Boy's little McDojo appears to be on an equal playing field with the legitimate grandmaster, Grandmaster Lee. It all boils down to excessive egos, money, greed, lack of honor and integrity, and feeling entitled!

After getting his bogus rank promotion and new title, "Grandmaster" John Boy starts to use his new rank and title in his marketing plan to bring in new students and his dojo starts to grow. His students believe that they are getting quality instruction from an actual respected grandmaster, totally naïve to the fact that their instructor is not a grandmaster at all, but rather a con artist.

And, as "Grandmaster" John Boy starts awarding higher and higher rank to his students, they become invested in defending their "grandmaster" against any and all who dare to question his legitimacy. Even if they see the truth of the matter, they still defend their "grandmaster" because they know that if he is proven to be a fraud, then that means their ranks are not legitimate either. When one domino falls, they all start falling.

This shell game continues for years and years, until the water is so muddied that the truth and the lies are too interconnected for anyone to figure out. Some martial artists know the truth, but when they speak about what they know, all of a sudden, they find themselves under attack by the members of this sham federation, in a desperate attempt to protect their own fraudulent grandmaster, and to save their own bogus ranks given to them by their so-called grandmaster.

Some of these martial artists have found out, after the fact, that their "grandmaster" is not truly legitimate, but they can't afford to admit it for fear of losing everything they have worked for. Others have no clue and are sincerely being loyal to someone who they consider to be a true grandmaster. Either way, the truth gets buried through years of covering up for this fraud and his organization.

So where does all of this leave us as far as these martial arts titles go? The answer is simple. It leaves us right where we started. Legitimate martial arts masters are humble, respectful, and give back to the martial arts world which they love. They are honored when others see them as a grandmaster, but that title is not the most important thing to them; their martial arts skills and continual self-improvement is what really matters to them.

Those who are not legitimate adore the title of grandmaster and demand that others call them Grandmaster when talking to them or referring to them in public, as they insist on getting their "due respect." They take themselves and their bogus titles way too seriously because most of the time, that is all there is to their martial art background.

Whenever someone requires others to call him or her "Grandmaster," "Supreme Grandmaster," etc., you can be pretty sure you are dealing with someone who is *not* a legitimate grandmaster.

I have martial arts titles which have been given to me by highly respected martial arts masters. One is an honorary title and the other is an official title. I also have a doctorate. But I never have, and never will, demand or require anyone to call me Shihan, Hanshi, or Dr. Sanders. When people ask me what they should call me, I simply tell them to call me Bohdi.

Legitimate grandmasters are more interested in their art, teaching others, and living life than they are in what everyone else calls them or thinks of them. They know who and what they are, and don't need constant praise or flattery to build up their ego, unlike those who acquire their titles through dishonest or questionable ways.

In the next chapter, we will look closer at the out-of-control egos which are so prevalent in the martial arts community today and how those egos are changing the martial arts world in detrimental ways. The water is about to get even muddier!

Look beneath. For ordinary things are far other than they seem.
The false is ever the lead in everything, continually
dragging along the fools; the truth brings up the rear,
is late, and limps along upon the arm of time.
Baltasar Gracian

Chapter 6
Out of Control Egos

Abandoning the ego is the secret of right living.
Taisen Deshimaru

I have touched on the out of control egos in the martial arts world several times in this book already, but I believe it would be helpful to look at this issue a little deeper. In this chapter, I will present evidence that shows without a doubt that there is an ego problem in the martial arts world, where there should be a spirit of humility, unpretentiousness, brotherhood, and helping each other.

Anyone who has been a martial artist for a while has seen the vast array of ways in which many martial artists continue to focus on their own egos instead of what the martial arts were meant to be. I am sure that pretty much every martial artist reading this book has seen the dishonest hacks who cross-promote each other, unscrupulous guys who self-promote or buy their ranks, guys who are selling online black belt courses or doctorates in martial arts, the "who's who in the martial arts" books, and of course, those ever so common pay-per-play martial arts halls of fame. Let's look at each of these in more detail.

Cross-Promotions

I have already touched on this dishonest practice, but will cover it in more detail here, as it is very applicable to this chapter. Cross-promoting is essentially the practice of starting a so-called martial arts federation or a so-called new art, and then the founders promote each other to the rank of 10th degree black belt and the title of grandmaster, neither of which the participants honestly earned.

This underhanded practice is more common than you might expect. The martial artists who use this scam, justify their actions by claiming that since they are the founders of such and such federation or a new system, they have the right to promote anyone to any rank or title that they wish. But the first step is always for the founders to cross-promote each other to the highest rank and title that they can, usually 10th degree black belt with the title of grandmaster.

Then, after they have declared each other to be 10th dans and grandmasters, they claim the right to promote anyone else to ranks up to and equaling that of their own. There is no testing, no working your way up the ranks, there is nothing other than these guys giving out worthless ranks and titles to those who are unwise to these scams and who have the money for membership and the applicable fees.

This simply is *not* how rank promotions are supposed to be done. I know the presidents of several legitimate organizations that complain about getting dozens of requests for cross promotions each month, where people from third world countries Facebook message them a 10th dan rank certificate image and expect them to return the favor. They quickly reply with a resounding no and then delete the message and block the person's profile to avoid further requests from them.

But there are many others who will happily accept the offer and still many others who create their own federation, and start the process anew with themselves at the top of the totem pole. The more students and black belts they get into their federation, or who they promote to a higher rank, the easier it is for them to claim legitimacy, even though they are anything but legitimate. There is power in numbers and they seek to build their membership as fast as possible.

After years of building their house of cards, it becomes increasingly harder for anyone to unravel all of the lies, false certificates, and fake ranks to get to the truth of the matter, which is that the whole organization was fake from the very beginning. The ranks and titles given out were not worth the paper they were written on.

But, after so many people have jumped on board and joined the federation, they each now have a personal stake in the federation not being exposed for what it truly is; so they all toe the line for the founders of this scam, defending them at every turn. After all, if these guys were proven to be frauds, that would make their own ranks and titles fraudulent, as I stated in the last chapter on titles, and they could never have that!

As the years go by and people throughout the martial arts world get used to calling these guys grandmasters, only those who knew them, and what they did all those years ago, actually know the truth. Everyone else considers them great martial artists, innovators, and grandmasters.

All they have to do is to weather the first few years and build up their fraudulent federation, muddy the water enough to where it is extremely hard for anyone to see what they have done, and recruit as many members as possible to add to their smoke screen. It is the ultimate martial arts con job!

Self-Promotion

This is very close to the practice of cross-promotion, but without the federation. These people are even too lazy to bother getting a buddy to start a federation with them, so they simply promote themselves to whatever rank and title they want. With today's technology, anyone with a few computer skills can make a certificate and print it out with whatever rank or title they want.

Of course, it is not worth the cost of the paper it is printed on, but that doesn't stop these frauds from doing it. Many times, these liars will claim that they were promoted by a famous martial artist who has already passed away. They figure that if they claim that a respectable and deceased martial artist promoted them, that nobody could prove them to be a liar.

They simply tell everyone the lie until they get enough people to believe them. And, if anyone does question them about their original lie, especially someone who knows the truth or knew the martial arts master in question, they change their story and claim that they never said anything like that, that someone made up that story. Their lies never cease, and most people don't seem to care enough to call them out on their dishonest claims.

In a previous chapter, I used the example of a martial artist who claimed that Hanshi Frank Dux promoted him to the rank of 10th dan. When I did some digging into the guy from this example, it turned out that he never got any rank over 2nd dan from *anyone*. He simply awarded himself a 10th dan and the title of grandmaster. Then he went to every event he could find and took photos with as many legitimate martial artists as he could to help make himself look legitimate. I even witnessed this fraud giving his best friend a 6th dan in Tae Kwon Do, even though this fraudulent "grandmaster" never practiced Tae Kwon Do himself.

Once these frauds promote themselves to a high rank and title, they always seek to give rank and titles to other people so they can muddy the water and claim to have other high ranking martial artists under them, just as this guy did. And round and round we go!

Buying Ranks and Titles

Other martial artists apparently look down on these scammers enough that they want nothing to do with these practices. Apparently, they believe that *buying* their rank and title from another martial artist will give them more clout and somehow make them more legitimate than the clowns who cross-promote each other or simply self-promote themselves to a higher rank. They are wrong!

These are people with lots of money and who are willing to spend thousands to purchase a worthless piece of paper stating that they have such and such rank from "Grandmaster Sellout." I know of people who have paid up to $6,000-$7,000 for a 6th dan rank, and even more for higher ranks.

This is so crazy to me that I can't even wrap my mind around it! Why would anyone in their right mind pay thousands of dollars for a worthless piece of paper in order to claim a fake rank? The lengths these people will go to in order to look like something which they are not, and to massage their massive egos, just blows my mind!

But, many people do just this. They have the money, they want the rank, and there is always someone willing to sell their honor for the right price. As John Webster pointed out, "Good gifts evermore make way for the worst persons." This should not be true in the martial arts world, but unfortunately, it is.

Not only will these people purchase fake ranks and titles, but there have been many who buy fake doctorates in martial arts as well. If anyone tells you that they have a Ph.D. in Martial Arts, they are lying to you; there is no such thing! But, just a few years ago, there was a guy who was selling a Ph.D. program in martial arts.

Apparently, you paid his price, and he asked you to write a "dissertation" for your program, which according to those who saw the program, was nothing more than a short research paper. You turned in whatever dribble you came up with, and voila, you get a worthless diploma stating that you now have a Ph.D. in Martial Arts.

The guy I used in the example above, who claimed Hanshi Frank Dux promoted him to 10th dan, also paid for his Ph.D. in martial arts. The funny thing about that is that everyone who knows this guy, knows he cannot write a complete sentence, much less a dissertation on any subject. I honestly don't think this guy could write a complete sentence if his life depended on it. But that didn't stop him from being awarded a Ph.D. in martial arts! It is all a part of the martial arts black market where you can get anything for a price.

The temptation to make money, a lot of money, selling ranks has unfortunately spread to some formerly legitimate organizations. One Korean based Hapkido organization is now famous for selling black belt rank and titles by mail order. The Secretary General of that organization searches Facebook for Hapkido schools and simply offers to sell the school owner rank from their organization without attending any training or even testing. 1st and 2nd degree black belt ranks can even be ordered directly from their website. What a disgrace!

Online and Distance Learning Black Belts

There are also several places which are selling programs where you get your black belt through video tapes and books. You simply buy their program, which will cost you a pretty penny, and then you video tape yourself doing the techniques from the videos. You send a video of yourself doing the techniques, and the guy gives you belt rank.

I know one guy, who claims to be a 14th degree black belt in Ninjitsu. He has been selling a distance learning course like this for years and years, and giving out black belt ranks. He also has several mystical courses for sale. This guy claims to be a spiritual teacher and markets himself as a spiritual/ninja master who has been all over the world and studied all spiritual traditions. And lucky you, he will teach you all his mystical knowledge, for a price, and you won't even have to leave your house to become a guru just like him!

There are quite a few of these distance learning scams out there. Now, I have no problem with distance learning. Most colleges now have courses and degrees available through distance learning programs. I have even taught online classes for a distance learning high school. They are great for those who need the flexibility that distance education allows. I have even completed some of my college degrees though online programs.

But, there is a huge difference between learning about business, education, psychology, etc., and learning self-defense or earning a black belt in a traditional martial art through a distance learning program. To learn true self-defense and martial arts, you need to work with a qualified instructor face-to-face, not learn from a book or by watching someone else do the techniques in a video. While experienced martial artists can learn techniques from videos, beginners need hands on experience.

In my opinion, getting a black belt through such programs is just a half step ahead of simply buying your rank. I guess, at least those who buy these programs are actually *trying* to learn the techniques, instead of simply paying for a piece of paper. In this case, it is the martial artist who is selling the program who is the scam artist, taking advantage of those who do not know any better or who do not have a place to learn martial arts. Always beware of anyone who is selling black belts through video courses!

Who's Who in the Martial Arts Books

This is another interesting way that some people use the overblown egos in the martial arts world for personal profit. I see these books over and over again. They have titles such as, *The 500 Best Martial Artists in the U.S.* or *Who's Who in the Martial Arts World.*

These books are about one thing and one thing only – the giant egos of martial artists in order to sell books. It is a pretty simple concept, and one that is even used on the parents of high school students and in other communities.

It works like this. Someone decides to publish a book titled, *The 500 Best Martial Artists in the U.S.* He then puts all the martial artists he can think of in his book and lets each of them know that they have been "honored" as one of the top 500 martial artists in the United States in the upcoming book, *The 500 Best Martial Artists in the U.S.,* which will be coming out next month.

He then lets each person know that he or she can buy as many copies as they want for their friends, family or students for only $60 each. The unsuspecting martial artist then feels so honored that he was included in this book that he immediately wants a copy so he can show people that he is considered "one of the top 500 martial artists in the country." Then he is able to use that book for marketing purposes for his dojo.

The publisher counts on the massive egos of the martial artists which he includes in the book to sell it. If each person in the book buys at least one copy, that would be a nice $30,000 profit, minus the printing cost, etc. That is a very nice profit made totally by preying on people's egos!

I saw one of these books last year being advertised on social media, and people couldn't wait to buy their copies of the book. I started watching as one person after another posted about being selected as one of the top martial artists in the U.S. When I started checking on some of the people included in this book, several were 1st and 2nd degree black belts, and there were even some included who were not martial artists at all! I don't know about you, but in my book, that is nothing more than a scam designed to profit off of the egos of martial artists.

A reasonable and prudent person would expect a "Who's Who" book to include those recognizable names from the industry or who give back to the martial arts community in some recognized way. But in most cases, these books are filled with names that just leave you asking yourself, "What the hell?"

Once this book came out, I saw another well-known martial artist, who runs a well-known event in New Jersey, advertise his own who's who in the martial arts world book. Hey, if there is money involved, there will be some hack willing to exploit people's egos in order to make a buck! What never ceases to amaze me is that people continue to fall for these scams over and over again.

As you can clearly see, many in the martial arts community obviously have issues with their egos. Whether it is cross-promoting each other to ranks and titles which they did not earn, self-promoting themselves, buying ranks and titles, or some other form of stroking their egos, many people's egos have spun out of control.

It is one thing to be self-confident in your abilities and to be proud of what you have accomplished. It is another thing entirely, to continually need positive reinforcement in the form of someone massaging your ego in order to make you feel good about yourself.

The latter shows a lack of self-confidence and a lack of humility. In most cases, this comes from the martial artist knowing deep inside that he did not actually earn his martial arts rank. In spite of all his accolades and his bragging about what a great martial artist he is, he knows inside his spirit that he does not have the skills he claims to have. He needs the awards and the recognition to soothe his tortured soul.

Still others may have earned their rank and title, and may indeed have the skills they claim to have, but they never did the internal work which a true martial artist should do. Therefore, they crave the

68

attention, recognition, and never-ending awards to feed their overblown ego.

There are plenty of unscrupulous martial artists out there who clearly see that many martial artists have issues with their egos, and they are more than willing to profit from that fact. No matter what your weakness may be, there will always be someone out there who is willing to profit from it, if you allow them to.

Albert Einstein wrote, "More the knowledge, lesser the ego. Lesser the knowledge, more the ego." And this definitely holds true in the martial arts. I have met many of the best martial artists of our age. And what I have found is that the best and most respected martial artists have the smallest egos. They are down to earth, caring, and always willing to help.

Their knowledge surpasses most other martial artists, but it never seems to go to their heads because their hearts, minds, and spirits are in the right place. They know what they have accomplished in the martial arts world, but they remain humble. These true masters have a gentle spirit about them. They are quick to smile and don't take themselves too seriously.

For example, when I was putting my two volume book series, *Secrets of the Martial Arts Masters*, together, I contacted Grandmaster Fumio Demura to ask if he would be willing to write a chapter for the first book. Grandmaster Demura graciously agreed to write a chapter for me on Budo. I had only met Grandmaster Demura once, but he remembered me and even remembered my wife and asked about how she was doing.

At the time, Grandmaster Demura was dealing with some serious health issues and was in his late 80's. I had mentioned in passing that I was having surgery soon. We did not dwell on this in the conversation; it was merely said in passing when discussing my timeline. To my surprise, after my surgery, Grandmaster Demura called me out of the blue. He called simply to ask me how I was doing and how my surgery went. I was completely honored by his concern and his phone call.

Here was one of the most respected martial artists of our generation, who was dealing with some serious health issues of his own and in his late 80's, and yet he made a point of not only remembering that I was having surgery, but to call me and ask how I was doing after my surgery several months later. That is the character of a true grandmaster!

I have found that true grandmasters have this kind of caring, giving spirit. You can see this when you speak to people like GM Fumio Demura, Sifu Al Dacascos, Doug Marcaida, and other true martial arts masters. They are comfortable in their own skin. As Einstein wrote, the more the knowledge, the lesser the ego. Those who are secure with who and what they are have no need to constantly massage their egos and to act tough. It is those with what Einstein called "lesser knowledge" who always seem to have the biggest egos.

There is another very common way that many in the martial arts community profit from overblown egos – the martial arts halls of fame. These scams are so prevalent that I have dedicated an entire chapter to them. In the next chapter, I will delve deep into these so-called martial arts halls of fame to show exactly how they work and why there are so many of them in the United States alone.

These are big business and prey on the egos of many unsuspecting martial artists each year. They are also a scam used by many martial artists who actually do know exactly what they are, but who do not care. Keep reading for an eye-opening journey into the world of the martial arts halls of fame!

The greatest enemies, and the ones
we must mainly combat, are within.
Cervantes

Chapter 7
The Martial Arts Hall of Fame Con Game

If you understand, things are as they are.
If you do not understand, things are as they are.
Zen Maxim

We have all seen the photos of the many martial arts halls of fame posted all over social media and how honored grandmaster so-and-so was to be "inducted" into this or that hall of fame. But do you really understand what these so-called martial arts halls of fame are and how they work?

Before I start explaining what these halls of fame are and how they work, I want to make something clear, as I can already hear my haters and detractors licking their lips, ready to attack me about my own hall of fame inductions. Yes, I have been inducted into several martial arts halls of fame.

I have always looked at them, and continue to see them, as nothing more than awards for my writing and contributions in the martial arts world. I accepted them in the spirit in which I thought they were given to me. Once I found out what they really are and how they truly work, I refused to accept any more hall of fame awards for which I was asked to pay money to accept.

I wanted to clarify the fact that, yes, I have accepted some of these hall of fame awards. I did so before I had an understanding about what they truly are and how they work. I thought they were actual awards when I accepted them. In reality, some were and some were not, but I accepted all of them in the belief that I was being honored. And, I was truly honored to be given recognition for my contributions to the martial arts at the time I accepted the awards.

Since then, my eyes have been opened to what *most* of these halls of fame truly are and how they really work. I say "most of them," because there are some that are truly martial arts halls of fame that are meant to honor martial artists for their contributions to the arts and they are legitimate. But there are many others which are nothing more than money-making scams, as I will explain in this chapter.

For example, last year, I was offered a "Lifetime Achievement Award" from a so-called martial arts hall of fame outside of San Jose, CA. I turned it down as I had found out what these so-called awards truly are, and especially this one in particular. Three months after turning down the "award," the guy who runs this so-called hall of fame started attacking me claiming that I am a "despicable fraud."

Imagine that! One day this so-called martial arts master wanted to give me an award as a great martial arts master and just a few days later, he wanted to destroy me as a despicable fraud. What was the difference? The fact that I found out who and what he was and refused to take part in his scam. Remember I discussed how these people like to control the spotlight, especially when they are afraid that the light may be pointed at them.

I have also seen this guy attack others that he offered his "hall of fame awards" to, a fact which is well-known by those who know about this guy and his so-called "hall of fame." That should tell you all you need to know about this so-called martial arts hall of fame. Unfortunately, his fake hall of fame is not the exception in the martial arts industry!

Another so-called martial arts hall of fame contacted me and asked for my permission to market my books on their website after "inducting" me into their hall of fame. I gave them my permission and was honored to be approached about them promoting my books to their members. At the time, I had another hall of fame award which I included on the cover of one of my books.

When this so-called "hall of fame" saw the other hall of fame on the cover, they contacted me all hot and bothered about it, and said they "could not put my books on their website because I was in a *competitor's* hall of fame." What! They contacted me and asked to use my books because they loved my teachings; and now, they are refusing to use my books because I am in a different hall of fame? Something sounded very fishy to me!

I responded saying, "I thought you were running a martial arts hall of fame, not a business. You sound like you are running a competitive business to me. Is this an actual martial arts hall of fame or is it a business?"

Their response was very enlightening to say the least. The president of this "hall of fame" stated, "It is a business! And by being in a competitor's hall of fame, you are promoting our *competition*. ALL martial arts halls of fame are a business!"

That is when it hit me! These halls of fame are not actually honors or awards, but rather businesses which are here to make a profit off of the egos of unsuspecting martial artists like myself. I promptly told them to remove my name from their hall of fame because I thought I was being honored, not paying for some plaque. Call me naïve, but in my defense, I am not the only one who has been conned by one of these money-making scams.

I had questioned the president of one of the other martial arts halls of fame earlier about the fact that people have to pay in order to receive their "award." He explained it to me like this, "We are a small organization and only charge what is necessary to cover the cost of the trophies and the dinners because we can't afford to cover the entire costs of the event ourselves."

Okay, that made sense to me. They are doing a service to help promote the martial arts and to bring martial artists together for some good fellowship and to recognize those who are doing good things in the martial arts world. I could see his point of view there.

However, after further investigation, I found that this guy runs his martial arts hall of fame several times a year in different locations around the country. The amount he charges people to accept their hall of fame "inductions" is much more than it takes to pay for the cheap plaque and $10 chicken dinner! All of a sudden, all of the explanations stopped making sense to me. This started to seem like nothing more than another business scam which preys on the big egos of martial artists. And I started doing more investigating and research into these so-called halls of fame.

What I found out was very enlightening, albeit disheartening. Most of these martial arts halls of fame, hall of honors, or whatever name they stick on them, are nothing more than businesses which are profiting from either the naivety of many martial artists or the colossal egos of other martial artists.

In my case, I was naïve. After my book, *Modern Bushido*, hit number one on Amazon, I was contacted by many martial arts halls of fame who stated they would like to induct me into their hall of fame. Before that, they had no clue who I even was; and likewise, I had never heard of any of them. None of these people had ever trained with me or even seen me do so much as a single kick, but they wanted me in their halls of fame.

On the other hand, some martial artists are not "accepting" these hall of fame "inductions" because they are naïve, but rather because they crave the attention. In fact, one hack brags about being "inducted" 66 times! He has been in the martial arts community for several years, so you know for a fact that he knows what these halls of fame are; he simply does not care as long as his ego is getting its yearly booster shot.

To talk to the people putting on these halls of fame, you would think they are doing a great service for the martial arts community. They will go on and on at length about how much work it is to put these events on and how they only do it because they love the martial arts. But when you do a little digging below the surface, you find that the reality is quite different from the appearance.

Alan Goldberg, who runs what he calls, "the largest martial arts hall of fame and awards banquet on the planet," was interviewed about why he does his Hall of Honors. The reporter asked, "Sir, what brings us here today?" His response was very enlightening. Goldberg stated, "I got to pay the bills." That doesn't sound like he is doing a service for the martial arts world to me; it sounds like he is making bank off of the martial arts community.

On Goldberg's registration form for his 2019 event, the form lists 43 categories for which a martial artist can be inducted into his Hall of

Honors. Then it goes on to state that the first 200 inductees will receive a free glass of wine. Wait...what! If you have only 43 categories and you are offering a free glass of wine to the first 200 inductees, how does that work?

Let's look at this a little closer. He has a category of "Master of the Year." If he has 43 categories and is giving awards to hundreds of people, does the award for "Master of the Year" really carry any meaning whatsoever? Does he have 75 "Masters of the Year" at his event? Something sounds a little fishy here!

Okay, let's assume he only has 200 inductees, which we know he has many more than that. With 43 categories, that would come out to be at least 4 martial artists in each category. That means that there has to be more than one "Master of the Year," "Grandmaster of the Year," "Martial Arts School of the Year," etc.

Now, stop and consider the fact that he has hundreds of people getting "awards" each year, but only has the 43 categories listed. Are these "awards" truly awards or are they simply a way of making money from the egos and/or naivety of the martial arts world? I think you know the answer to that question.

To be "inducted" into Goldberg's *Hall of Honors* it will cost you $249 if you are a *first time inductee*, $215 if you are a previous inductee, according to his 2019 registration form. This leads us to the question, "Why would someone need to be inducted into the same hall of fame more than once?" If you are a martial arts hall of fame inductee, do you need to renew your induction over and over again or do the people who buy into this charade simply need more and more hall of fame trophies to pacify their overblown egos?

If you are inducted into the Pro Football Hall of Fame or the Pro Baseball Hall of Fame, even the best of the best is inducted only once. If you are inducted into a hall of fame, you are a hall of fame inductee, period. You don't have to be inducted over and over again. We only see people being inducted over and over again in the martial arts world. Why do you think that might be? The answer is obvious – MONEY and EGO!

Here is how these so-called martial arts halls of fame work. Anyone can start a hall of fame. Most of them make arrangements with a hotel for a discounted group rate on the rooms and to use the hotel for the awards ceremony and dinner. The "inductees" pay for their own rooms and each one pays a price for their dinner and trophy.

Although the people putting on these halls of fame state that the fees are to cover the cost of the dinner, trophies, hotel, etc., the fees are usually much more than the cost of a cheap chicken dinner and the cheap trophies which are given to the inductees. The cost runs anywhere from $175-$250 on up.

The dinners that I have seen would normally cost you about $10 and the trophies may cost anywhere from $20-$30 depending on the style, etc. Then they have the cost of the banquet room from the hotel which is usually not that much. Some halls of fame don't even bother to use a hotel; they simply hold their so-called award ceremony in their little strip mall dojo with a few cheap, foldout metal chairs. (Talk about classy!) So their cost may run around $50-$60 per inductee.

But wait, don't forget about family members and students who will most certainly want to be there to support their instructor, husband, wife, or friends. They also have to pay anywhere from $150 on up just to attend and get the cheap chicken dinner. Even if we give them the benefit of a doubt and say they spend $75-$100 per person, which they absolutely do not, they are still raking in the money!

In addition, there are fringe benefits for the guys who put on these so-called halls of fame. They pay for movie stars and martial arts celebrities to attend their event in order to make them look legitimate and for marketing purposes. Then they use these celebrities' names as a way to convince martial artists to take the bait and shell out the money for their awards. After all, if Joe Super Star is attending, it must be a legitimate hall of fame, right?

Furthermore, both the guys putting on the hall of fame and the inductees get to take photos with the martial arts celebrities. These photos are then used to market their dojos to prospective students and parents who may be looking for martial arts instruction. When they see the photos of the inductee with this celebrity or that celebrity, it looks very impressive to prospective students or parents who are looking for a legitimate dojo to learn martial arts.

The whole thing is a pay-per-play game where the person who puts on the hall of fame gets to take publicity photos with celebrities and the martial artists who are being inducted into their hall of fame and make a name for themselves. And, of course, the hack who puts on the hall of fame gets to rake in a very nice profit to boot. If this sounds like a pretty sweet deal to you, you would be right. As Alan Goldberg said, "Gotta to pay the bills."

Many of the martial artists who get sucked into these events are like I was, simply naïve about the way these things work. They are contacted through the mail or on the phone and told that they have been nominated to be inducted into the martial arts hall of fame for their contributions to the martial arts. It is absolutely normal to feel honored by such an offer, especially if you are not in the loop about how these events work.

Others are simply in the "good ole boy" club. These are the people you see at almost every event, over and over again. It is like a little martial arts fraternity. These same men and women are inducted over and over again. They get to break out the tux and fancy dresses and use the occasion as a big photo op to market themselves across the martial arts world and to stay in the limelight.

These people know how these hall of fame scams work, but simply do not care. Some of them are being paid to be a part of the events, and others are more than willing to shell out a few hundred dollars to hang out with their buddies and get some great publicity photos. It is a fairly cheap way to market yourself and get photo ops with famous celebrities.

Many of the celebrities who attend these events know that some of the people putting these events on are as fake as a $3 bill, but they don't seem to care. Some of them get between $5,000-$10,000 plus all expenses paid to attend these events. I don't hold that against them at all. Hey, if someone is going to pay me $5,000 to stand around and take photos with strangers and visit with my friends for a few hours, I am all for it.

Where I think it crosses the line between getting paid for your celebrity status and doing something a little shady is when you know that the guy putting on the event is shady or even a complete fraud, but you go there and lend your name to the event anyway. In my humble opinion, this is supporting a con artist and a fraudulent hall of fame scam.

But hey, that's me; I do realize that my standards are higher than many other people's standards, but I believe that, as martial artists and good human beings, we are supposed to put our integrity ahead of our bank account. But what do I know? I am just an old guy from Colorado who writes books on character, honor, morals, and philosophy.

There is one martial arts hall of fame which puts on 9-10 martial arts halls of fame a year! How can those truly be special hall of fame awards when they average almost one event each month of the year? Again, I think you know the answer to that question.

Another issue with the martial arts halls of fame is that there are so many of them. How is it that there is one football hall of fame, one baseball hall of fame, one basketball hall of fame, and even one rock and roll hall of fame, but the martial arts world needs dozens and dozens of them? Once again, the answer will sound like a broken record – MONEY and EGO.

Several martial artists who attend these gatherings state that they are not interested in the trophies or awards, but rather they just go for the fellowship and to see old friends. I can understand that. I have greatly enjoyed seeing some old friends and meeting new martial artists at these events. It is good to get together with friends and other martial artists.

On the other hand, I could hold a weekend get together where everyone comes just to visit, see old friends, and enjoy good fellowship, and no one would show up. I would hear things such as I don't have the money, money is tight, I am busy that weekend, etc. But, if I called it the Rocky Mountain Martial Arts Hall of Fame, gave each person a cheap trophy and a $10 chicken dinner, people would gladly pay me a couple hundred dollars, plus pay for their room and plane ticket to get here.

What would be the difference? The latter would stroke their egos. Whereas, just getting together to visit and enjoy each other's company just doesn't carry the same weight as being inducted into another martial arts hall of fame, being able to brag about being inducted into the hall of fame, and using the whole event to promote themselves across social media.

If all this wasn't bad enough, they have even created "Youth Awards" where they *sell* "hall of fame awards" to children. Yes, you read that right. They *sell* awards to children and unfortunately there are enough parents from the participation trophy generation who are willing to do this; it has become more common than you might think.

If you are paying for your award, it is *not* an award; you are simply buying it. A true hall of fame induction should not cost you anything, other than what it costs you to travel to the event and your hotel room. Therefore, those who participate in these sham events are, in actuality, buying themselves martial arts hall of fame trophies.

And again, I don't hold this against most of the martial artists who get sucked into this. They accept their awards with an honest heart and truly believe they are being honored.

Hey, even the best of us get conned from time to time. The key is, once you see the con, don't keep allowing yourself to be fleeced. Don't allow your ego to talk you into paying for anymore so-called "hall of fame inductions" when you know it is nothing more than a money-making scam run by questionable martial artists and even outright frauds. Remember, if something seems too good to be true, it usually is.

The bottom line, when it comes to these martial arts halls of fame, is that if you are paying $175-$250 or more to be inducted, you are not being honored, you are buying a product. You are paying an exorbitant price for a bland chicken dinner with canned vegetables and a cheap trophy, period.

To make matters even worse, I have seen the hacks who put these fake halls of fame on each year, actually turn around, get upset with someone, and kick him or her out of their hall of fame after the person has paid for their trophy. They are "inducted" into whichever shady hall of fame it may be, paid for their "induction," and then when the owner of the hall of fame turns against the inductee, he decides to kick him out of his hall of fame.

This is like going and buying yourself a $250 membership to an exclusive club, and then the club decides to kick you out a month later without refunding your money. All for no other reason than the owner decides that he doesn't like you. This happens all the time in these fraudulent halls of fame. They are a joke and a rip off, not real martial arts halls of fame. They are simply a pay-per-play business gimmick.

In the next chapter, I will take a closer look at martial arts federations and what they are all about. As I have alluded to in earlier chapters, there is power in numbers. That is why people join fraternities and different organizations, and that is why there are new martial arts federations started each year. But there is much more to many of these federations than meets the eye, as you are about to find out.

Hold yourself responsible for a higher
standard than anyone else expects of you.
Henry Ward Beecher

Chapter 8
Martial Arts Federations

To every man there opens a high way and a low way,
and every man decides the way his soul will go.
John Oxenham

If you put the words "Martial Arts Federations" into the Google search engine, you will come up with 8,840,000 results. Wow, that is almost nine million results when searching for martial arts federations. That's a lot!

Do we really need another martial arts federation? Well, I think you can answer that just from those search results. Why are there so many martial arts federations in the world today? The answer has to do with both power and money.

Not all, but many federations give out rank and titles to members in one form or another. Some make outright promotions and others will take someone's certificate and transfer their rank and title into their federation, giving the person a new certificate with that same rank and title, but from their federation. Actually, I shouldn't say "giving" them a certificate, as they do charge them a nice chunk of change to put their stamp of approval on their rank and/or title.

This is another way that dishonest martial artists are able to take their fake certificates and parlay them into a "real" certificate from a "recognized" federation or organization. Essentially, they take a fake certificate and trade it in for one that *appears* to have some validity.

I said "appears to have some validity" because the vast majority of these federations don't seem to do much in the way of vetting these people. They simply take their word for it, see a copy or photocopy of the certificate, and give them their stamp of approval, for a price of course. Basically, they are a willing participant in the scam, either by negligence or by simply not caring one way or the other.

It is not that the federation itself is necessarily bad, although some definitely are, but when the members do not vet who they allow in, they find that deceitful martial artists can and will use their trusting nature against them. And since most federations charge for membership, they look at the numbers and the money more than they look at the character of those martial artists they allow to become members.

There are so many martial arts federations out there that unscrupulous "martial artists," can absolutely find one somewhere that will enable them to continue to lie about their credentials and to make themselves appear legitimate. Just pay your membership dues and you're in.

Most federations are about cliques, money, and power. There is power in numbers. I have already discussed how some dishonest martial artists will start a federation and promote themselves to a high rank and title. This is something that anyone can do, although it is blatantly dishonest.

But just starting a federation and giving yourself a fake rank and fake title is meaningless unless you build your federation up. (Actually, it is meaningless, period, but I am referring to their underhanded strategy.) They have to recruit members in order for their federation to look legitimate. The more members they have, the more legitimate their fake rank appears.

I know of one federation started by a couple of hacks several years ago. These two were constantly stating how they were going to be millionaires from their federation. They had plans to sell memberships, do rank promotions, and publish books and training DVD's, and more. It turned out that both of these guys had substance abuse problems and criminal backgrounds. Their personal issues soon destroyed their dishonest business venture.

However, before their fake federation crashed and burned, they both cross-promoted each other to the rank of 10th dan and the title of Hanshi, but their rank and title were both seen as bogus, not only because it was, but also because they could not complete their scam and make their federation look legitimate. Thankfully, they were only able to con a very small handful of people and their scheme fell apart, as all of the legitimate martial artists who were suckered into being a part of this federation quickly resigned and left.

For any martial arts federation to be useful, they have to have a good number of members. Building the federation up serves several purposes. They can then give rank and titles as they see fit without anyone questioning them too much. Basically, they have a little fraternity where the members defend each other if someone does call them on their dishonest practices. They pretty much cover each other's butts.

The more members they attract, the stronger they become, and the stronger they become, the less likely any other martial artists will call them out on their fraudulent practices. After a few years of building their federation membership and brand, the water becomes so muddy that nobody even considers the fact that the founders cross-promoted each other instead of actually earning their ranks and titles. Then they are home free, for the most part.

I must point out that I am talking about the dishonest martial arts federations here. There are also many legitimate organizations which are honest, well-run, and which actually do care enough to vet potential members.

In life, you will find that there is good and bad in every community, whether it is the martial arts community, the legal field, the medical community, etc. That is just life. There will always be dishonest people of low character and people who live their life with honor and integrity.

There are good, honest federations, and there are dishonest federations with alternative, hidden agendas. As with most things in life, when it comes to martial arts federations, it is buyer beware.

I did a lot of my training one-on-one with Shihan William Jackson, and as so, I didn't get to see all the political garbage in the martial arts world until my martial arts books and writings became very popular. Then I got firsthand lessons concerning many of the things which I discuss in this book.

My eyes were opened to how many of these federations work, how crooked and dishonest many in the martial arts world are, all the cliques, the personal attacks on other martial artists, the martial arts trolls, the frauds in the martial arts world, the focus on money, the backbiting, etc. I have to say, it has been very disheartening to see all this garbage in a community which is supposed to be based on character, brotherhood, and honor.

And even with a ridiculous number of martial arts federations out there, I see new federations being started every year. One has to wonder why the martial arts world needs anymore federations. Now, when I see a new federation, I always look below the surface for the real reason it is being formed.

After I became so disheartened by what is going on in the martial arts world, I decided to distance myself from all organizations and federations. I resigned from the ones that I was in and have declined to join any others since that time. This doesn't mean that the ones I was a part of were bad or dishonest. I simply decided it was best to go back to being a loner and independent from any organizations.

During a conversation with my friend, Dana Abbott, Dana stated that he is independent of all the martial arts cliques and organizations. He stated that he always makes up his own mind about people in the martial arts and never listens to the gossip and negative talk. At the time, there was a shady group of hacks who were trying to turn Dana against me with lies and misinformation. His words struck a chord with me and I decided to follow his path where this is concerned. I proceeded to resign from any federation that I was a part of and left it at that.

I have found that being a part of a group has both its advantages and disadvantages. When you are part of a federation, others connect you to the members of that organization, which can be either a good thing or a bad thing, depending on the quality of the members.

If the organization is full of real, legitimate martial artists of upstanding character, it can be a very useful membership and can provide both good advice and support for you. The members will back you up when others try to attack you, and the years of martial arts wisdom and knowledge can help you learn and advance in your martial arts training.

But, if the membership is littered with dishonest or questionable members, it will reflect badly on you. Even if you do not know those members and have nothing to do with them, your enemies or haters will use the fact that you are in the same organization as those questionable members, and they will use it to cause you problems.

Since my books started becoming very popular in the martial arts community, I have had various scumbags attacking me about one thing or another. They spin the truth, make things up, and outright lie about me to try and destroy my reputation. They will take things I say out of context and use anything possible to hurt me and my family.

Because of the constant attacks, I have honed my self-defense skills to a sharp edge. I am more careful about everything I say and do in order to avoid giving my haters anything they can try to use against me. Essentially, my haters and enemies have helped me by teaching me how to better keep myself safe and unassailable.

I now know more about what to look for when it comes to martial arts scams, dishonest martial artists, all the ways they con people, and how they scheme to attack other martial artists. Because of this, I have decided to stay away from the martial arts federations. I am constantly offered this rank or that rank from different federations, and I turn them all down.

More often than not, I find that the new federations, and a lot of the older ones, are nothing more than scams. There is one that I know of in California which gives out the title of "Grandmaster" in Kajukenbo to people who never even practiced Kajukenbo. It is a disgrace!

There is another completely fake federation based out of Seattle which exists only on paper. The fraudulent "grandmaster" who runs this scam has a graphic designer make nice looking certificates and cons people into joining his non-existent federation.

The martial artists on his so-called "board of directors" are constantly changing, as he will con a group of people by asking them to be on his board of directors. Then after a few months, they realize they have been conned and that there really is no actual federation, and they leave. Then he starts all over again with a new group of people.

This same guy carries a fake badge and claims to be everything from a gourmet chef, a graphic designer, a grandmaster, a war hero, and even a "living legend." The problem is that he is none of those things! They are all lies which come from the twisted mind of a martial arts con man.

I have to admit, I wasn't surprised when one of my readers sent me a link about this guy last week. Apparently he was being investigated for sexual assault on a lady who hired him for a $35 private self-defense lesson. This guy is a real piece of work, and yet many people in the martial arts world have no idea about this stuff and continue to call him a grandmaster. It truly is pathetic!

I know of another martial arts federation which was started about a year or so ago. One of the founders called me and said that he really wanted me to be a member. Membership was around $300 and I knew enough about one of the other founders that I didn't want anything to do with it.

It was only active for a few months when I talked to the martial artist who asked me to join. I asked him how his new federation was going and was informed that he was no longer a part of it; he was filing charges against his partner for fraud and questionable financial dealings.

The guy who I mentioned in an earlier chapter who claimed that Hanshi Frank Dux promoted him to 10th dan and that he has a Ph.D. in martial arts, actually started his own federation as well. This guy loves to name drop, and he was adding many martial arts celebrities' names on his board of directors, many of these people had no idea they were being advertised as being a part of his federation. He even had my name on his list as a board member, until I demanded that he remove it. It was simply another martial arts scam.

I could go on and on concerning the horror stories from different martial arts federations, but I think you get the point. If you want to join a federation, more power to you, but I stay far away from them now. I have no problem walking my martial arts path alone at this stage of the game and do not have the time or energy to be involved in any organization.

As I stated earlier, these federations are often about money, power, and influence. I discussed how they bring in money through selling membership, books, DVD's, etc., and how there is power in numbers. They use their numbers to cover up for each other and to back up questionable members, as well as hit back whenever someone attacks the organization for things which might not be on the up and up.

In addition, they use their numbers to build influence in the martial arts world. Many federations also have their own martial arts halls of fame, tournaments, and events. With more members, they acquire more name recognition; with more name recognition comes more influence in different parts of the martial arts community. They become like a fraternity or a martial arts clique and wield a certain amount of power when it comes to things such as black balling other martial artists from certain events or from membership in other organizations.

If it sounds a little like dirty, gotcha politics which we see played out every day in Washington, D.C., there's a good reason for that – that is exactly what it is. Federations can be very political and can influence many martial artists through their little cliques.

Think about it. They are not running an organization just for the fun of it. It takes time and money to put a martial arts federation together and to run it. If you are thinking of joining a federation, always do your homework! Investigate both its reputation and its membership; remember the old truism, others will judge you by who you associate with.

In the next chapter I will look at these martial arts cliques and how they work in more detail. Many of them are not unlike different mafia families in the way that they do business and try to control people in the martial arts world. In fact, I call them martial arts mafias because that is exactly how some of them conduct themselves. I think you will find this information very eye-opening.

Perceive things which are not obvious.
Miyamoto Musashi

Chapter 9
The Martial Arts Mafias:
Behind the Scenes Cliques in the Martial Arts

Never exchange a good conscience for the
good will of others, or to avoid their ill will.
Charles Simmons

When I talk about cliques in the martial arts world, I am talking about groups of martial artists who have formed an informal group or alliance for the sole purpose of controlling other martial artists in one way or another. These people use a variety of underhanded techniques to lift some martial artists up and to put others down, depending on their devious objectives.

Some of the common practices they use are starting malicious gossip, personal websites used to libel martial artists not in their clique, actively black balling martial artists, using internet forums and social media in malicious ways, falsely claiming certain martial artists are fakes and frauds, and using the internet as a weapon against those they dislike or want to destroy. While some of these may sound innocent enough, trust me, they are anything but.

The people in these cliques are like an evil prayer chain. Christians use a prayer chain to spread the word that someone needs help and needs people to pray for them. Overall, they have good intentions and a desire to be helpful. One person will call several other people and let them know, and those people each call other people, and so on down the line. Then they all pray for the person who needs help and support him or her.

People in these martial arts cliques, or martial arts mafias as I call them, use a phone tree in the opposite way; they use it not to help people, but to try to destroy them. When these malicious little trolls dislike someone or someone doesn't bow down to them like they want them to, they start calling people in their clique and spread lies and malicious rumors about him or her. They understand the power of malicious gossip when it is spread throughout a community.

These people are experts at lying, slandering, libeling, and attacking people's character. These cliques have the "go to" guys at the head of their phone trees. They call these mentally challenged gossips first and drop some new piece of gossip which they "just learned about." Then the rumor mill goes into high speed, blowing people's phones and emails up as fast as possible, spreading the new "information" about their target.

Of course, the "new information" is totally false and made up, and these people know it, but that doesn't stop them from using it to accomplish their objectives. Their objectives range from getting someone to fall in line to trying to totally destroy someone's reputation in the martial arts world. These people are purely narcissistic, evil liars, but, as with many narcissists, they know how to con people into believing that they are upstanding martial artists who only want to get the "truth" out there.

The truth is that these cliques are made up of evil, malicious, backstabbing people. They get some kind of rush from believing that they have the power to make or break other martial artists. And if you watch them closely, you will see that they are always doing this in one form or another. Once they tire of personally attacking one martial artist, they quickly move on to their next target in a never-ending loop of malicious attacks on other people's character or martial arts prowess.

They will attack one martial artist for weeks or months, until they believe they have done enough damage, then they move on to the next guy on their hit list. All the time, acting as if they are doing the martial arts community a much needed service by "outing the frauds." It is nothing more than character assassination conducted by a group of malicious fools.

And the kicker is that the people who are involved in these cliques actually *are* the fakes and frauds! Some of these people run fraudulent martial arts halls of fame. Others run fraudulent martial arts federations. Many of them have completely fabricated martial arts backgrounds and have used many of the underhanded techniques I have already discussed in this book.

90

They are those who cross-promote each other to higher ranks, who promote themselves, who lie about their rank and title, and some are not even martial artists at all, but complete frauds. Others are well-known in the martial arts world and have lost their way due to their over-blown egos and narcissistic tendencies.

Here you might be wondering why these people would risk doing all this stuff when it might backfire on them if people find out the truth about their own martial arts backgrounds. The answer to this is pretty simple. If they control the spotlight, they can keep it from shining on them.

Think of it this way. The magician in a magic show always tries to misdirect your attention to where he wants your attention to be. If he is doing the trick with his right hand, he works hard to get you to watch his left hand or his pretty assistant. And while your attention is on the lady in the skimpy costume, the trick happens right in front of you, but you fail to see it because your focus was somewhere else.

This is the same technique that these malicious con artists in these cliques use. They know that they must keep your attention off of their little house of cards in order to keep people believing the lies that they have made up about their own martial arts background – their fake ranks, fake titles, their underhanded activities, their internet troll activities, and their out-of-control egos, all of which are contrary to being a true martial artist.

What is the easiest way for them to do that? They control the spotlight and keep it focused on other martial artists, calling them the fakes and the frauds. They get people riled up and focused on everyone else, while they keep their dirty little secrets safely hidden in the darkness, far away from the spotlight.

And when someone does attempt to expose their lies, their fraudulent claims, or their malicious, spiteful deeds, they immediately jump into action and start calling their phone tree to spread lies about that person in order to discredit him or her before people start to believe the truth.

This is not some new technique which is unique to the martial arts world. Cults use this technique all the time. If a member leaves the cult and is exposing the truth, the first thing they do is attack that member's character and try to discredit him or her. This is why many cults try very hard to get damaging information on their members, even if they have to falsify it.

For example, the NXIUM cult, which has been in the news a lot lately while I have been working on this book, would take new members and video tape them saying personally damaging things about their family. If they had nothing bad to say, they simply had them make up stuff such as my father abused me. It did not matter if it wasn't true. All that mattered to them was that it was personally embarrassing or injurious, both to the woman and to her family.

They would have them submit to taking very explicit, nude photos of themselves to go into their file, photos they would never want anyone else to see. They even required them to add new damaging information to their file on a monthly basis just to remind them that they had this collateral on them and that they would use it against them if they tried to leave or discussed what was happening in the cult. Basically, these things were used as a form of blackmail to get these women to do whatever the cult wanted.

These martial arts cliques work in much the same way, but without the collateral. If someone tries to reveal the truth about them or makes them upset in some way, they actively try to destroy his or her reputation. Since they have their system down to a vindictive art, they quickly trash that person's reputation so no one will believe what he reveals about them.

They use several methods to do this, but they always start by blowing up people's phones with calls and text messages in order to spread their malicious lies and gossip. Then they move on to social media, martial arts forums, and websites.

In no time at all, they have launched an all-out war against the innocent guy who found out the truth about them. They muddy the water so fast that no one in the martial arts world knows what or who to believe, but since these people have well-known connections, many lean towards believing them. After all, why would Grandmaster Super Star be friends with these people if they weren't on the up and up, right?

In doing this, they consistently keep the spotlight off of themselves, while at the same time, they are able to attack and brutalize the reputation and character of anyone who they dislike or want to bring down. It is an extremely devious and dirty game.

As I said, these malicious cliques use various methods to accomplish their objectives and keep their deeds in the dark. The first step to successful self-defense is knowing what weapons your enemy may use against you. One of those weapons is the use of the internet to spread gossip and lies.

Using the Internet as a Weapon

Next to spreading malicious lies and gossip in person, over the phone, and through email, the preferred weapon for these malicious individuals is the internet. These pathetic trolls love to use social media, forums, and websites to spread their lies. The reason for this is that, deep down inside, these people are cowards.

Many of them are so cowardly that they even use fake names and fake profiles while doing their dirty work. They do this because they know that if people actually saw their true character and what kind of things they really do, they would lose all respect for them, so they try to maintain a very low profile. Several of the people who run martial arts halls of fame have been caught using fake profiles to harass and spread false rumors about other martial artists, as well as other halls of fame. It really is dirty politics!

There is one hack in California who was using fake social media accounts and fake cell phone accounts to attack martial artists who he disliked. This guy also runs a fake martial arts hall of fame. This guy is constantly using technology to attack other martial artists. He is a real piece of work! The worst part of this is that other martial artists know he does this, but still support him.

This guy has absolutely no morals whatsoever. He was caught attacking another martial artist who has dementia, both on social media accounts, over the phone, and through fake cell phone texts. It doesn't get any lower than attacking someone who is dying and using his disease against him, but that is the kind of people who are participating in these cliques.

Many of these people have dozens of fake social media accounts. You can block them under their real profile, but that doesn't stop them from stalking you online or attacking you from any of their fake accounts.

One woman who runs a shoddy martial arts website and who is known to use her website to attack other martial artists who she doesn't like, actually attacked me on Facebook. She was extremely rude and obnoxious, so I blocked her. Almost immediately, she started spamming my Facebook pages with lies about me and my character. She did it all with a new account which she made for the sole purpose of harassing me, after I blocked her original account.

It only takes a few minutes for these dishonest people to make a fake account on social media. They are professional stalkers and internet trolls. Many of these people spend much more time harassing people online than they do training or working. It truly is pathetic that anyone would use their short time on earth in such despicable ways!

Here is how these people work the internet to accomplish their objectives of smearing other martial artists' reputations in order to try to ruin them in the martial arts world. First, they will make up lies and rumors and get them spreading through their personal connections. They do this through a few phone calls, texts, and emails.

Then they embark on their internet campaign. They will write malicious articles and post them on various websites, forums, and social media, where they start to be shared by other social media pages, etc. They also spend quite a bit of time sharing these lies and misinformation through their fake social media accounts, pretending that it is some shocking news which they just discovered.

They have lists of every martial arts forum, martial arts social media pages and groups, and they plaster their libelous lies and rumors all over them in an attempt to get as many other martial artists as possible to start bashing the target of their lies. We have all seen how dishonorable and ignorant "martial artists" start to pile on and attack a martial artist when they read this garbage. It truly is a spectacle unworthy of any true martial artist!

The more places they can post their lies, the faster the lies spread among those martial artists who lack the intelligence to discern the truth from the lies. They will spend, not days, but weeks and months doing this to the people that they target. Some are so obsessed that they will do this for years and years in a malicious attempt to destroy someone's reputation.

Now, ask yourself, "What true martial artist would ever spend months or years trying to destroy another martial artist for their own malicious purposes? I think you know the answer to that one – NO true martial artist would do this!

It is amazing that anyone ever believes the lies which they post all over the place, but there are a lot of martial artists out there who are not savvy enough to see through the scam. These con artists will even post stuff under ridiculous fake names, which should be an obvious signal to people that their articles and posts are nothing more than malicious lies.

Even though they write stuff under these fake names and user accounts, many people are not intelligent enough to comprehend the fact that this should be a major red flag that something is not on the up and up. And this is what these internet bullies count on. They count on people being stupid enough to, not only believe their lies, but to spread them on their own social media accounts and through gossiping. It is amazing the number of people who will believe information being posted by people using obviously fake names and profiles!

I mean, how stupid do you have to be to read an article by someone who signs his name as Monkey Butt Boy or King of the Haters and actually believe what you are reading has any validity to it whatsoever? It never ceases to amaze me how gullible some people are.

Most real martial artists would never believe the stuff written by malicious cowards who are too spineless to even sign their real names to their dribble, and the martial arts mafia knows this. But they also count on the gossip spreading wide enough to achieve their malicious objectives. While they know that intelligent people would never believe their lies written under made up names, they also know the power of gossip. This is one reason why martial artists should be very careful repeating things they hear or read on the internet.

Let's look at a scenario. You see some bogus article written online and just scan through it, not taking the time to consider why it is written or even noticing that it is written by someone who signs an obvious fake name to the article. Then you mention to your buddy that you saw this article on the internet about Master Smith.

Next, the martial artist, tells another martial artist that he heard from *you* that Master Smith is a fraud. All of a sudden, the story takes on a new persona. It is not just some bogus garbage written anonymously online, but it came from *you*, a well-respected martial arts master.

Then the next guy repeats it, using your name, which gives the false information more credibility. And this pattern continues, which is what these dirty martial art cliques count on. And now *your name* is connected to the liable and slander being spread about Master Smith. You have just become a willing, albeit unintentional, accomplice to libel, slander and defamation of character, which is exactly what the people in the clique wanted.

You have been unknowingly used by these martial arts mafias to give credibility to their underhanded strategies, simply because you innocently repeated their lies to one of your buddies. It really is a devious and twisted strategy that these cliques use to destroy their competition or anyone who they dislike and want to bring down.

Directing the Spotlight

Many of these cliques apparently declare themselves to be the martial arts police. They publicly proclaim that they are here to expose the fakes and frauds in the martial arts world. As I have already discussed, the purpose for this is two-fold – to destroy those they dislike or who they see as competitors, and to keep the spotlight off of themselves.

First, they try to convince other martial artists that they are only trying to expose the frauds to help the martial arts world. They make themselves out as if they are doing the martial arts world a favor and should be praised for taking the time to expose those they deem not worthy of being real martial artists.

Then they try to keep people's attention focused on those people by actively stalking everything that these people say or do. They stalk them day and night, attempting to find anything they can twist or spin to use against the unsuspecting target. They will take comments out of context. They will Photoshop photos. They will even fabricate emails or messages from these people with photos from their social media accounts, and then make fake screen shots and post them as proof that Master Smith is a fraud.

I have actually seen them do all of this and much more in malicious efforts to destroy someone's reputation or to hurt their business. They try to constantly keep the spotlight on their lies about Master Smith until others in the martial arts world really don't know what to believe about Master Smith.

These cliques like to control the spotlight in order to make sure it never gets pointed towards them, as I discussed previously. They do this because they know that their own fraudulent martial arts background could never stand up to the scrutiny. Because of this, they are constantly gossiping, posting "new information," and keeping the libelous lies and slander circulating throughout the martial arts community, without most people ever suspecting that these guys are truly the martial arts frauds that people should be distancing themselves from.

This chapter has touched on just some of the main ways that these martial arts cliques attempt to control people in the martial arts community. After my books became popular, many of these people befriended me. I had no idea about all of this stuff or how these people work; I learned all of this from watching how they work and seeing firsthand their deceitful tactics.

They absolutely do conduct themselves like the old-time mafia guys, that is, without actually killing people. Instead of killing people, they resort to trying to murder people's reputations. And just like the mafia bosses, those at the top are pulling the strings. They prefer to keep an honorable reputation themselves, so they are very careful about how they conduct themselves in public.

They try hard to keep their distance from the dirty business of spreading lies and rumors, and instead, they have their lackeys do their dirty work. They know exactly who to go to in order to get false rumors, lies, and gossip started. They simply make a few phone calls and then sit back and watch as their lies spread throughout the martial arts world.

And even though they started the lies and defamation themselves, when others come to them with the information, they act shocked to hear it, or they may casually reply, "Yes, I heard that too. I am so disappointed to learn that Master Smith is a fraud." Then they smile to themselves, knowing that their plan is working just as they planned it.

I have seen these people use these dirty tactics over and over again. Many of these puppet masters are people who are very connected in the martial arts world, and some are just losers with no life. Attacking other martial artists somehow makes them feel less pathetic about their own lives and gives them the feeling of being important in some small way.

Those who are connected actually use the pathetic losers to do their dirty work. They know who they are and how they think. They understand that these people have no life, no morals, and that they love spreading gossip and lies; so they use that knowledge to accomplish their goals of bringing down their enemies or their competition.

I know of one of these scumbags from New York who even uses his connections in the New York City Police Department and with criminal biker gangs to intimidate anyone who may try to expose him or come against him. A threatening phone call from a police officer or some gang member is much more than the average martial artist wants to deal with, and this is exactly what this well-known piece of garbage counts on. The more you know about these people, the more they truly resemble a mafia organization!

I could give you specific names of many of these people, as I have been researching them for several years now. I know who many of them are and exactly how they work. I even have recordings of several of these guys spreading their gossip about other martial artists, and amazingly, about each other. They even explain how they attack others. Believe me, these people are not innocent martial artists who enjoy gossiping; they know exactly what they are doing, and they have their disgraceful practices down to a fine art.

Several of these guys actually started turning on each other a year or two before this book was published. At that time, I didn't know what I know now about these people. Because of my books and teachings, and the fact that I have a large following in the martial arts community, these people were trying hard to befriend me. I guess they figured if I bought into their lies and published them on my blog or social media pages, their gossip would spread quickly.

Each of these factions got in touch with me to rant about the others. I am sure that I was just one out of dozens of phone calls they made during that time, trying to turn me and everyone else, against the other guys and make themselves look like the good guys.

As a result of their little war against each other, I was able to listen to their rants, watch their actions, and learned exactly how these people work. They each explained in detail how the others used these tactics to destroy people and gave me specific evidence of them doing so.

They each claimed the others used this tactic or that tactic to destroy people that they disliked, and now they are doing it to them. But it didn't take long to see that they were *all* using these tactics that I have discussed in this chapter and that they had *all* used these tactics many times to go after those that they wanted to bring down.

I have recordings of these guys attacking each other and spilling the beans about what they have done and how they did it. It is amazing how they threw each other under the bus at the drop of a hat, but that is what malicious people of low character do. Mobsters turn on each other and murder each other; these martial arts cliques turn on each other and try to destroy each other's reputations. It is the same concept, just used in a different way to accomplish different objectives.

I have never been one to bow down to anyone, much less people I do not respect. A couple of these people wanted me to jump when they snapped their fingers, and I put them in their place, as I have been known to do from time to time. That wasn't acceptable to them and it wasn't long until these people turned on me as well. They started spreading lies and false rumors, even trying to turn my best friends against me.

At that time, I let them know that I have recordings of their phone calls and that I had a boat load of evidence about who and what they truly are and what they have done. Immediately, I started getting messages and phone calls threatening to sue me if I went public with the recordings or mentioned their names. These people went into panic mode, as they knew that those recordings would open people's eyes to who these so-called "martial arts masters" truly are and what they do behind the scenes.

I have never been one to back down from bullies. When they started spreading lies about me, I hit back and hit back hard. And when I did, people from all over the martial arts world started contacting me and telling me how these same people did the same thing to them. That is when I really started to see the extent of this problem and how bad these people really are. They have been doing this stuff for years and years!

Other martial artists started sending me evidence of these people doing the same exact thing to them. I received screen shots, text messages, emails, and even emails from some of these guys' instructors who no longer want anything to do with them. I even received emails written by the family members of some of these guys, telling me about how their brother completely lied about his martial arts background and his education. It was shocking!

The more research I did on my new attackers, the more I found out that they were the real martial arts frauds! Some of them had promoted themselves to the title of grandmaster. Some of them promoted their friends to the title of grandmasters. Some claimed to be grandmasters of Kajukenbo, but never practiced Kajukenbo in their lives.

The more I found out, the more obvious it was that each and every one of these guys was as fake as a three dollar bill and as malicious as a mafia boss. Several of these people are very well-known individuals in the martial arts world! People just took their claims for granted and never took the time to look behind the façade.

These people have ruined many lives in the martial arts community by spreading lies and false rumors, and they did so maliciously and purposely. And, what's more, I found out that many people in the martial arts community did actually know about these people's fraudulent background and fraudulent activities, but never stood up to them out of fear of them using these same underhanded tactics against them.

Many martial artists simply decided to "go along to get along." When I found this out, I was dismayed. Martial artists are supposed to be men and women of honor, courage and integrity; and here I was, finding out that many who I used to look up to were simply spineless cowards who didn't have the backbone to stand up against these cliques because they feared that these people might use the same tactics against them.

I had martial arts friends who told me, "Don't be too hard on them. They are just scared because they know what these people do and they are scared that they will do the same thing to them." Maybe so, but they lost my respect. I don't cower down to anyone for any reason. Even before I started martial arts, my father taught me to never back down from a bully; I never have.

So imagine my disillusionment when I found out that many martial artists, who I had respected, cowered down to these people instead of having the courage to do what was right and stand up to these martial arts cliques. It appeared that many martial artists chose to sell their honor for another worthless hall of fame trophy or free publicity, instead of standing up for what's right. This is something I just can't understand!

I know one martial artist who calls himself a grandmaster, who was befriended by one of these people. I considered this guy a friend and I let him know everything that I knew about this dishonest fraud and the underhanded things he was doing, but he continued to support him. I finally gave up on the "friendship."

A couple of months later, a mutual friend called me and told me why this guy had refused to listen to me and continued to support this martial arts fraud. He informed me that the fraud, which runs one of the fake halls of fame, actually paid this guy thousands of dollars! I already knew that the guy who runs this hall of fame paid certain celebrities thousands of dollars to show up to his event, so when he told me this, it all made sense.

It never ceases to amaze me how many people are willing to sell their honor and integrity for a little bit of money or even a cheap glass trophy. I had warned my "friend" about this con man many times, and each time he assured me that he knew that Master X was a fraud and that he knew about the underhanded things that Master X was involved with.

When I asked him why he continued to support him or to go to his fake hall of fame, he simply said that he was trying to help him get his life straightened out. On the surface, this sounded like a nice thing to do, although I warned him how many others had tried to do that very same thing, only to have him turn on them. He refused to listen to me no matter how many times I warned him about Master X.

Master X invited this guy to his black belt test at his dojo, and my buddy went. He called me after that test and told me that he was embarrassed to have been there and that this guy had no clue what he was doing. He said it was so bad that he could not sign off on any of the certificates.

At that time, Master X was holding a fake rank of 6th degree black belt in Tae Kwon Do. I say that the rank was fake because it was given to him by his best friend who does not even practice Tae Kwon Do. How do you give someone a rank in a martial art which you do not practice or hold rank in? You simply print a fake certificate and promote him to whatever fake rank you choose. These people do that all the time.

I asked my buddy how he thought someone could be a 6th degree black belt and not know how to run a black belt test. He simply stated that he knew that Master X was fake, but he was trying to help him do better. While I agree that we should help people as much as we can, when you see someone who is conning people, he doesn't need help, he needs to be put in his place.

I continued to talk to my buddy about this guy and warned him over and over that being so closely connected to this fraud would affect his own reputation which he was trying so hard to build up.

When I found out that my buddy was taking money from this hack, I was greatly disheartened and ended our friendly relationship. I have no time for those who are willing to sell their honor for a handful of money, or for any other reason as far as that goes.

Several of the guys in these cliques have several million dollars in the bank. Having that kind of money, no morals, and a willingness to use that money to destroy or manipulate other martial artists, is a very dangerous combination. People who are morally bankrupt, but have lots of money, can do a lot of damage to innocent people. We see this all the time in the criminal underworld.

Hopefully, you now have an idea about what these underground cliques do and how they accomplish their malicious goals. They are completely void of any honor or integrity, and in my book, that alone means that they are not true martial artists. Whatever happened to honor and integrity in the martial arts? In the next chapter, I delve deeper into this question.

The man of principle never forgets
what he is, because of what others are.
Baltasar Gracian

Chapter 10
What happened to Honor and Integrity?

I have seen the best karate.
All that really matters is what
kind of human being you are.
Masami Tsuruoka

What happened to honor and integrity in the martial arts? Honor and integrity were extremely important to the old Asian masters, but these traits seem to have been forgotten by many in today's martial arts world. A well-renowned martial artist defined honor and integrity in the following way.

In the martial arts, we typically define honor as high respect, great esteem, and adherence to what is right for a conventional standard of conduct. It can also be seen as regard with great respect or to fulfill an obligation or keep an agreement. As martial arts students, we demonstrate honor by honoring our teacher with great respect and fulfilling our obligation to our training by adhering to the code of conduct. As martial arts teachers, we demonstrate honor by honoring our art and teaching with an ethical standard that sets an example for others to follow.

For a martial artist, integrity should mean the quality of being honest and having strong moral principles. A martial artist should live their life with a high level of integrity. Integrity is a character trait that is admired as being unwavering and strong. It shows wholeness of character.

As martial arts students, we demonstrate integrity by showing faithfulness and loyalty to our art. You should never betray a friend's trust even if it causes you problems. As martial arts teachers we demonstrate integrity by being fair in our treatment of all students with the understanding that each student has different needs. We hold each student accountable to the strict standards of conduct, training, and leadership within our school.
Grandmaster Richard Hackworth

When I ask what happened to honor and integrity in the martial arts, don't get me wrong, there are still many martial artists out there who take character, honor, and integrity seriously. I have thousands of readers who absolutely try to live by a strict code of honor and they give me hope for the future of the martial arts and the younger generation of martial artists.

On the other hand, there are quite a few, like those I have referred to in this book, who appear to not give honor or integrity a second thought. Their lack of honor is blatantly obvious by their actions. They have forgotten what Master Funakoshi taught, "The ultimate aim of karate lies not in victory nor defeat, but in the perfection of the character of its participants."

This famous quote by Master Gichin Funakoshi is not being widely taught in the modern martial arts world where the focus is more on mixed martial arts, tournaments, flashy kicks, and gymnastic style displays. The teachings on character, honor, philosophy, and the spiritual side of the arts have largely fallen by the wayside; they simply aren't being taught anymore to the majority of martial arts students.

Even among older martial artists, I see many saying things such as, "All that philosophy stuff is bullshit. It is a waste of time and has never saved anyone in a real fight." Well, for those who understand the true philosophical teachings of the martial arts, that statement is highly debatable at best.

The philosophical side of the arts is where we learn when to fight and when not to fight, how to de-escalate a possibly explosive situation, how to control our mind and emotions, and much more. In short, it is very much a part of true martial arts and should be integrated into every martial arts class.

Teaching someone martial arts without integrating teachings about character, honor, integrity, courage, and philosophy is actually a dangerous proposition. You are teaching people dangerous techniques without giving them any guidance about how they should and should not be used. As Master Hwang Kee stated, "All they want to learn is punching and kicking. This is not martial arts, it is only fighting."

This said, most dojos I have seen do not spend time teaching their students lessons on character traits or philosophy. They may go through the motions when it comes to certain character traits such as bowing to show respect when coming into the dojo or leaving the dojo, but is there any true respect being taught?

For example, I have seen many dojos in which the kids will give a quick head bob for a bow before getting on the mats. This is done so quickly that it almost appears as if someone simply smacked the student in the back of the head. There is no thought given to this action; there is no true respect in merely going through the motions without actually involving the mind in the action.

The mind is vitally important when it comes to the martial arts, whether we are talking about showing respect or any other aspect. If you recall, in an earlier chapter I referred to students screaming at the top of their lungs in place of a traditional kiai. The kiai is supposed to be used to focus one's energy into whatever technique is being used. Do you really think that the students who are screaming at the top of their lungs are focusing their energy into that kiai or are they simply screaming as loudly as possible in an attempt to influence the judges and win the kata competition?

What makes the difference is whether or not the mind is engaged in focusing their energy. Screaming is simply going through the motions and has no true meaning or purpose, other than to impress the new generation of tournament judges who have forgotten what a kiai is supposed to be.

The kiai, on the other hand, has a specific purpose, and it is not simply for show. It actively engages one's energy and focuses that energy into the technique, making the technique much more powerful. Comparing a real kiai with the screaming I see in today's tournaments is like comparing apples and oranges.

Likewise, there is a huge difference between the quick, silly, head bob bows I see so often today and a true bow which comes from a place of deep respect. The difference is not just a physical difference in the two bows, but comes from a reverent mental attitude of respect, as compared to simply going through the motions. Respect comes from deep inside, not from a simple, mindless action; it must originate from the spirit.

These are just two examples that I see where students are taught the actions, but there is no internal substance to go with the action. It is simply going through the motions without any true understanding of the meaning behind the action.

The same can be said for teaching honor, integrity, or any other character traits in the dojo. The instructor can't just quickly mention them in passing and expect the students to internalize the traits and make them a part of their life. They must be taught in a way in which the students internalize the traits and integrate them into their whole life, not just think about them in the dojo.

Moreover, the majority of dojos that I have seen never address character training to start with; they work on blocks, punches, kicks, falls, katas, etc., but they don't take the time to teach character traits, meditation, and the true meaning behind the martial arts.

I will go even further and state that the vast majority of instructors were never taught these things either. How could they possibly know that these traits need to be integrated into their classes when they were never taught to them to begin with? You can't teach something you don't know.

As traits like honor and integrity fall by the wayside, they become forgotten by the instructors and students alike. As more and more dojos become sports oriented, the focus is turned more towards winning the next tournament or competition, instead of being focused on the perfection of one's character.

When I started writing my books on character, honor, integrity, etc., I was shocked at the letters and emails I received thanking me for my teachings. I was especially shocked by the letters and emails stating that they had never heard teachings like that before. I couldn't believe that so many people in the martial arts had never heard what I was teaching before!

The fact that so many martial artists had not been taught much about honor, character, integrity, and loyalty is alarming to me. They were being taught how to fight, or more accurately, how to spar in a tournament, but not the mental or spiritual side of the arts.

Let me be perfectly clear, there is much more to the martial arts than learning how to fight or defend yourself. You can teach a dog or a rooster to fight, but that doesn't make them martial artists. True martial arts training must be a combination of spiritual, mental, and physical training – spirit, mind and body. Without all three of these, your training is unbalanced and incomplete.

Think of these three aspects as the three legs of a stool. If you only have the physical leg, the stool will not stand up and is of no use. The same goes for having only two legs; the stool just tips over. All three legs are important for the stool to be useful, and all three must be balanced or the stool will be shaky.

If you only have the physical aspect of the martial arts, you are missing 2/3 of your training. The prisons are full of people who know how to fight, but don't have the mental stability to control their emotions or the spiritual training to know how to swallow their pride and walk away from a fight. If you are only teaching your students the physical side of the arts, you are doing them a great disservice. Martial arts students need balanced instruction which teaches them, not only how to fight and defend themselves, but how to live.

When we make winning the most important thing, then honor and integrity automatically take a back seat. When students see their instructor cutting corners when it comes to his integrity, then they learn to do the same. Honor is not a trait which one obtains by accident; it must be taught and perfected by consistent practice. It must be lived daily. It must be a part of your being.

Consider the people in the martial arts cliques and those who have achieved their rank and titles by dishonest means. Most of those people either have students or used to have students. Do you really think that they taught their students about honor and integrity? Did they teach persistence or did they teach their students how to bend the rules to their advantage? Did they teach their students that honor is more important than appearances?

Again, you can't teach something that you know nothing about or that you don't live yourself. If these people are willing to lie, cheat, deceive and manipulate people, to put their ego ahead of what is right, and maliciously try to destroy their fellow martial artists, how do you think they are going to teach their students to be men and women of honor and character? Would you want these people teaching your children?

I know that I look at things quite a bit differently than many people, but I believe that if you are going to teach martial arts that you have a giri, a moral obligation or duty, to teach the arts in a way that they are useful in all aspects of everyday life, not just in the extremely rare event of a physical attack or simply for sport.

Many instructors do not teach about morals, character, honor, or integrity simply because they prefer the physical side of the arts and believe that the students should learn these other things on their own time. Other instructors do not see these teachings as politically correct, especially in our culture. Even our schools no longer address most of these subjects. They see right and wrong in subjective terms and do not feel comfortable teaching their personal morals to others.

I know many instructors who no longer teach meditation because they do not want to offend parents who may not understand what meditation truly is. They are focused on keeping students in their dojos and walk a fine line between teaching what needs to be taught and keeping the parents happy.

Larger dojos have classes that are between 45 minutes to an hour long. They want to get the students in, get them stretched, work on a couple of techniques or do some kata work, and then get to the next class. These instructors see no need to "waste" time teaching character traits, meditation, etc. After all, their students are there for exercise and sport, not to learn all that philosophy stuff, right?

The more the martial arts world moves away from teaching character traits, honor, integrity, and morals, the more we are going to see martial artists who are willing to compromise their honor for higher ranks and titles. If you don't take your honor seriously, you will always be willing to sell it for a price. And if you are willing to sell your honor, you will always find a buyer in the martial arts world.

We need to get back to teaching character traits, honor, integrity, and morals in the dojo. We need to be willing to teach our students right and wrong, and not just how to fight or how to win. We need to give our students the tools to live a successful life, not just teach them another sport or hobby. We need to be teaching them warrior ideals, not some watered down semblance of the martial arts.

When I started writing about character, honor, integrity, and other character traits, I didn't do it for money or fame. I started out by hand writing my teachings in two large journals for my sons to have and to treasure after I am gone. The more I wrote, the more I thought to myself that these teachings are something I would buy in the book store, so I took a chance and sent my manuscript off to several publishers.

To my surprise, after sending my teachings to four publishers, I got two offers back and my teachings ended up being published. From there, I started teaching deeper truths about character, honor, integrity, etc. and integrated my teachings with my martial arts beliefs. Soon I developed a following in the martial arts world.

Now my books and teachings are used to help teach young people all over the world. Many martial arts instructors use my books to teach their students about character, honor and integrity. Regardless of whether instructors use my books or other teachings on character training, it absolutely needs to be taught in every martial arts dojo.

When we get back to teaching our students, not only how to fight and defend themselves, but how to live the warrior lifestyle and how to integrate good character, honor, and integrity into every aspect of their lives, then we will see more honor and integrity in the martial arts world. We have to teach the younger generation because they are the future of the martial arts.

In the next chapter, I will discuss what the lack of warrior ideals in the martial arts means for the martial arts world and our students. It is time to get back to teaching students the warrior mindset!

True Budo has an overwhelming emphasis
on the development of moral character.
Glenn Morris

Chapter 11
Lack of Warrior Ideals

*The way of a warrior is based on humanity, love
and sincerity; the heart of martial valor is true
bravery, wisdom, love, and friendship.*
Morihei Ueshiba

There are many different styles of martial arts, but there are only
two kinds of martial arts – martial arts meant for self-defense and
self-improvement, and sports martial arts meant for fun, recreation,
and competition. These two kinds of martial arts, although they are
both spoken of as martial arts, are as different as night and day.

Asian martial arts were originally brought back to the United States
after World War II when military men coming home from the war
brought back some of what they learned while they were in Asia.
These men were mainly focused on the self-defense aspect of the
arts. They had seen how the Japanese used both their hands and feet
as weapons and brought these arts back with them to America.

Although martial arts tournaments soon followed, the main focus
was on self-defense and developing hard core fighting skills which
could be used in the streets. Some had knowledge of the internal arts
and some did not, but all understood their importance as far as the
warrior mindset was concerned.

Today, it seems that the vast majority in the martial arts world have
forgotten the true warrior mindset. Most martial arts dojos are now
focused on the sports and hobby practitioners, with little if any
attention given to the true warrior arts. There are probably many
reasons for this, but most stem from the desire to use the martial arts
to make money.

Many of the hard core warrior teachings and techniques are not
appropriate to teach to young children; I know I would not teach
them to my young students when I was teaching martial arts.
Children's minds are not mature yet and, as we all know, they tend
to not think things through and to make bad decisions at times.

A responsible martial arts instructor doesn't want to teach dangerous techniques to those who are not mature enough to handle that kind of information responsibly. You don't want to be the instructor who taught a 14-year-old boy lethal techniques, only to later find out that he killed someone in a playground fight. That would be a sickening feeling to say the least!

The vast majority of martial arts students today are under the age of 18. Therefore, martial arts instructors have two choices – either conduct extensive vetting of their students, which would cut into their financial bottom line, or water down the martial arts which you teach to your students, not teaching them the brutal truths of the martial arts. The latter is what the majority of instructors opt for in the Western martial arts world.

Because of this, the majority of commercial martial arts dojos have lost the true foundation of the martial arts – the warrior ideals which the martial arts evolved from in the beginning. This has fundamentally changed both the underlying purpose of the arts and the warrior mindset in the arts.

When I talk about losing the warrior mindset in the martial arts, most people automatically think of the more brutal techniques, and those are definitely a part of the warrior mindset when it comes to the physical side of the martial arts. But there is another side of the warrior mindset which they overlook – the warrior ideals. The warrior lifestyle is not all about fighting.

Throughout the centuries, true warriors have lived by a higher code than the average person. They held themselves to a higher standard. Not only were they experts in the art of hand-to-hand combat or self-defense, but they also sought to improve themselves in every way – spiritually, mentally, and physically. This included working to perfect their character, living with honor and integrity, developing courage and wisdom, self-control, and other character traits which are lacking in many dojos today.

Today, many dojos do not take the time to discuss or teach morals or character traits; the focus is mainly on watered down techniques, katas, and light sparring. After all, how much can you truly accomplish in a 45 minute or one hour class when trying to keep kids in line?

If your lesson is on joint locks, one hour is a very short amount of time to warm the students up, teach the correct technique, warn the students about the importance of going slow to avoid injuries, have them partner up and practice the technique, give feedback, corrections, etc., and still have time to get into a deep discussion about morals and character.

This goes back to the fact that the focus for most of these dojos is on making money. When you have a set class schedule, you must get the students in, warm them up, present the lesson, practice, and get them out in time for the next class to start or for them to be picked up by their parents. This is how a business works.

Most instructors seem to expect the students to develop their views on morality and character training from their parents or somehow mysteriously acquire this knowledge on their own. Maybe they will obtain this information from movies, movie stars, or the current popular music celebrities, but somehow, I don't think they will learn good morals or character traits from any of those sources.

The warrior lifestyle is a phrase that I coined years ago to refer to living a complete, balanced lifestyle based on the warrior ideals. This lifestyle includes true martial arts, self-defense, and a focus on the perfection of character, honor, integrity, meditation, spirituality, and self-improvement in every area of your life – spiritually, mentally, and physically. It leaves nothing out; it is a balanced lifestyle based on high standards and a code of ethics based on warrior ideals.

Since this book is not about the warrior lifestyle, I won't get into detail about all that it entails here. If you are interested in learning more about the warrior lifestyle, get some of my other books which explain in detail exactly what this lifestyle entails and how to live it to the fullest. I would suggest reading *Modern Bushido: Living a Life of Excellence* and *Bushido: The Way of the Warrior*.

The point of this chapter is that the warrior ideals are rarely being taught in modern martial arts classes today. This trend of moving away from true, warrior martial arts to a watered-down version of the arts, has led to many of the problems in the martial arts world today.

Those interested in living the warrior lifestyle are not interested in appearances. To these people, buying rank or titles is the height of hypocrisy and idiocy. After all, no piece of paper or long piece of cotton is going to save your life if you are attacked by a violent predator. No fake martial arts hall of fame trophy has ever saved anyone's life. Warriors know that an overblown ego will get you killed in the streets.

All of the issues with the martial arts community, which I have listed in this book, are directly opposed to true martial arts and the warrior lifestyle. They are based on nothing more than hollow appearances and cheap marketing schemes, neither of which have anything to do with true martial arts. True martial arts must be based on honesty and sincerity.

Think about it. Do you truly think that teaching students watered down martial arts is preparing them to defend themselves from a vicious attack from a cruel predator or experienced street fighter? Are cool looking gymnastic moves going to save their lives in the streets?

The vast majority of the martial arts students in today's Western culture are not being taught good morals or character traits, nor are they being taught useful self-defense techniques which could save their lives. If you take these teachings out of the martial arts, what's left? The answer is simple – a fun hobby or another recreational sport.

Here I need to make something perfectly clear. There is absolutely nothing wrong with participating in martial arts as a fun hobby or for a sport. Why would there be anything wrong with that? Just as there is nothing wrong with playing tennis, football, baseball, or practicing yoga. There is nothing wrong with participating in martial arts as a hobby, even though this is not what true martial arts are for.

The problem lies in the fact that most of the martial arts dojos market themselves as a school that teaches self-defense, develops discipline and good character. They market themselves as if they are teaching true martial arts from a warrior perspective, when they really aren't. And those who do not know the difference, have no idea that they are not being prepared to defend themselves.

If you have never studied martial arts and have no idea about what a true martial art is and what it is not, how would you know that the martial art you are being taught is watered down or that you are really not being taught true self-defense? You don't.

To compound the problem, many instructors have no other martial arts instruction besides what they have learned in these same watered down dojos. They have never been in a real fight in their lives and honestly know nothing about real self-defense and what it truly means. They were never taught about warrior ideals or good character traits, so how could they pass these qualities on to their students?

True martial arts and sports martial arts have very little in common. Just look at some of the characters portrayed in the sport of MMA, which is becoming one of the most popular martial arts. Could you imagine those guys teaching someone about morals or good character traits? Not from what I have seen!

A great example of this comes from one of the most popular martial arts movies of all time, *The Karate Kid*. In this movie, Mr. Miyagi and Daniel portray the character traits of true martial artists, whereas, the Cobra Kai dojo portray what happens to kids who are taught how to fight, but not about morals or the internal side of the arts.

And just like in the movie, if you teach kids how to fight, but not when or why to fight, you are most likely training bullies or kids who will get themselves into trouble one way or another. If you are going to give someone a dangerous tool or skill, you should, at the very minimum, teach them when it is appropriate to use that tool or that skill.

As a martial arts instructor, you have a responsibility to make sure you prepare your students to be able to truly defend themselves and teach them all that goes with those dangerous skills. This includes teaching how dangerous those techniques are, de-escalation techniques, how to control their emotions, how to control their ego, and giving them the character traits that will enable them to live a successful life. Martial arts are about much more than learning how to fight or compete!

The problems we are seeing in today's martial arts world come from martial artists not living their lives according to true warrior ideals. They put their egos ahead of what's right. They put hollow appearances above developing true skills. They put marketing and money ahead of developing men and women of character, honor and integrity. They give students a distorted sense of self-confidence which could actually get them killed if they ever had to defend themselves in a life-or-death situation.

After decades of the martial arts being a free-for-all, where people fake their ranks, their titles, buy fake martial arts hall of fame inductions, and more, just think of how difficult it must be for parents or potential students to find an instructor who will truly teach them the ways of the warrior. It is so disheartening.

These instructors have lost their way. They have forgotten, if they ever knew, the way of the warrior. They have sold their souls for fame and fortune, and left Budo, the martial way, for a quick buck and hollow, meaningless appearances.

They have taken the martial arts down a dark, murky path littered with fraudulent claims, ranks, titles, and bogus teachings, and hall of fame scams. The martial arts world desperately needs to clean house and turn back to the ways of the warrior, back to developing men and women of character. Martial artists need to start living the warrior lifestyle and stop pretending.

118

The old martial arts masters would not teach just anyone who came to them and asked to learn their martial art. And even with those who they did agree to teach, they would not teach them everything that they knew until they were convinced that their character was good and trustworthy. Character was extremely important to them.

On the other hand, they did not teach for a living, as so many instructors do today. If you are trying to get as many students as you can, it doesn't make sense to turn away prospective students. Therefore, most instructors today will teach anyone who can pay for their monthly lessons, character be damned. In the end, it all boils down to priorities.

I have brought this up to many instructors today. When I point out that they should consider the character of the students before arming them with dangerous techniques, I can't tell you how many excuses I have heard to justify the fact that most of them teach anyone who wants to learn how to fight.

The justification that I hear most often is that, "The martial arts develop good character, so I am helping this student or that student become a better person." Well, on the surface, this sounds like good logic. If you are taking a thug and changing him into an upstanding citizen, how could that be a bad thing?

The question is, how are you changing his character when you are not taking the time to teach good morals or good character traits. If you are moving students in and out in one hour intervals, twice a week, I have news for you, unless you are very unique, you are not spending enough time on the warrior ideals to make a lasting change in their lives, as far as their character goes.

I am all for helping as many people as I can to become better people, but it doesn't just happen magically because you teach them martial arts. It takes a lot of time and dedication to your students. And I have news for you, the strip mall McDojos which teach students twice a week for 45 minutes to an hour, are not making those lasting changes in students' lives. You must instill those traits into your students and, as any parent knows, this takes a lot of work.

In addition, many of these classes are no longer even taught by the martial arts master who owns the dojo, as he or she is too busy running the business. Advanced students run the majority of their classes for them, students who were never taught the warrior ideals to begin with.

The problems in the martial arts world can be likened to a weed in your garden. If you have a noxious weed in the garden and you don't take the time to remove it, its roots grow strong and it produces thousands of seeds. Those seeds scatter and before long your garden has been taken over by weeds. The flowers or vegetables which were meant to flourish in the garden can hardly be found, as the weeds have taken over and are everywhere.

This is what has happened in the martial arts world. The warrior ideals have been largely forgotten, replaced by watered down martial arts, fraudulent practices, fake martial arts masters and grandmasters, and very dubious practices. It is harder and harder to find a dojo which teaches true martial arts today or even gives lip service to the warrior ideals on which the martial arts were originally based.

So how would a student who has only trained in sports martial arts switch to learning the true martial arts that include the spirit, mind, and body philosophy and all that goes along with the warrior lifestyle? The warrior lifestyle has very little to do with sports oriented martial arts.

Consider the following quotes about the sport of football. A college football coach once said that "Winning is not the best thing, it is the only thing." Another opined that, "There is no second-place winner." All sports, including sports martial arts, are based upon competition. No matter what spin some apologist tries to put on it, the goal of sports, is winning. There is the winner, and then there is everyone else.

In true martial arts, the measure of success is, have you done your best and are you constantly working to improve yourself? If you can answer yes to both of these questions, whatever you have accomplished has been honorably and nobly achieved. The warrior lifestyle is about constant, never-ending self-improvement. You are not in competition with anyone else; you are simply striving to be a better person than you were the day before.

Miyamoto Musashi stated, "Study strategy over the years and achieve the spirit of the warrior. Today is victory over yourself of yesterday; tomorrow is your victory over lesser men." Think about that. Today is victory over yourself of yesterday. What does this actually mean?

In the simplest of terms, this means that you are constantly in a struggle to be a better person today than you were the day before. Never stop trying to improve yourself. Always strive to move closer and closer to the perfection of your character. This is the idea behind the philosophy of the Japanese term kaizen, which loosely translates as constant, never-ending improvement.

The warrior lifestyle is not a lifestyle based on fighting, although developing the skills to defend yourself when necessary is absolutely a part of this lifestyle. It is actually much more than that. It is a balanced lifestyle that prepares you to excel in every aspect of your life – spiritually, mentally, emotionally, and physically. This is the difference between true martial arts training and sports martial arts. Sports are something played for fun, recreation, and competition; the warrior lifestyle is a way of life.

Just think about how different the majority of martial artists would be if they were taught the warrior lifestyle with a focus on constantly improving themselves in every way, instead of the vast majority of their focus being on how to fight, score points in sparring competitions, or how to win in forms. If we taught our students correctly, they would not only be able to win in competition, but they would be doing so with honor, character, and integrity; they would become better human beings in the process.

Please do not see this as an attack on sports martial arts. There is a time and a place for everything. Tens of thousands of people enjoy sports martial arts, and there is absolutely nothing wrong with that. I am simply trying to show the distinction between true, traditional martial arts and sports applications. Both have their place in the martial arts world. Furthermore, the warrior ideals should be a part of the students' instruction no matter which type of martial art they are interested in learning.

In the next chapter, I will discuss why the martial arts have gradually moved away from teaching the warrior ideals and have gravitated more towards sports oriented arts. This will help you understand how the martial arts have morphed into what they are today.

*Since karate exist for cultivating the spirit
and training the body, it must be a moral
way surpassing mere techniques.*
Masutatsu Oyama

Chapter 12
How did this Happen?

The world is a dangerous place,
not because of those who do evil, but
because of those who look on and do nothing.
Albert Einstein

There are several reasons that the martial arts have moved away from the ways of the warrior. Since the martial arts world is totally unregulated in any way, it has become a free-for-all. As I pointed out earlier, there are no set standards for the martial arts; each style or system has its own standards concerning belt rank, titles, techniques, teachings, etc.

This gives unscrupulous martial artists the chance to pretty much do as they will. With the advancements in technology, they are armed to the teeth with ways to con both perspective students and other martial artists.

True martial artists look at these people as a total joke. They know that they are frauds, and they are the butt of many jokes, but this knowledge, and those jokes, do nothing to stop them from scamming people across the martial arts world. When true martial artists don't care enough to get involved to stop fraudulent martial artists from taking advantage of others in the martial arts world, who will?

From what I have seen, most true martial artists are too busy with their own lives to worry about the frauds being perpetrated on the martial arts world. They figure that the truth will come out eventually, so they just focus on their own lives, and classes.

But, just like with the weeds in the garden, if you don't keep your garden weeded, the weeds will take over; just ignoring the weeds won't make them magically disappear. You have to actively remove them from your garden and keep them from spreading their seeds of destruction.

This has not happened in the martial arts world. The frauds and scammers have been left alone to do what they will. I am sure that in the beginning, there were only a few, so no one truly cared too much. They simply had nothing to do with the frauds and figured they would fade away.

As their scams became profitable, and others saw that there was money to be made by running fake martial arts halls of fame, faking their ranks and titles, etc., more and more of these people started selling out and engaging in fraudulent activities. It is never wise to turn a blind eye to wrong doing!

This "leave well enough alone" attitude has enabled dishonest martial artists to pretty much do as they please. And after decades of these people teaching others and muddying the water, their seeds have spread widely.

The organizations who declare themselves to be the watchdogs for the martial arts world, are usually run by the very same con artists that they proclaim to be watching out for. (I already discussed how these people try very hard to control the spotlight and keep it off of themselves.) These people use their websites, forums, etc. to point their fingers at others, but in reality, it is nothing more than a weapon used to hurt innocent martial artists, at least for the most part.

To make matters worse, these fraudulent organizations who claim to be "outing the martial arts fakes," have gained a big enough following of ill-informed and thoughtless martial artists that other martial artists are actually afraid of being targeted by these borderline criminals. They are afraid of being attacked by these con artists who use the internet as a weapon to destroy the reputations of true martial artists. Talk about letting the weeds take over the garden!

This persuades even more true martial artists to simply ignore these people, keep their heads down, and focus on their own lives and students. Which, in turn, allows the frauds even more freedom to continue to perpetrate their dishonest practices on the martial arts world even further, as too many in the martial arts world are now afraid to stand up to them. This has become a vicious cycle which is quickly spinning out of control.

This cycle has allowed the frauds and McDojos to get a strong foothold in the martial arts. And, it will take a lot of unity and work to remove them and to bring the martial arts back to what they once were and what they are meant to be.

Martial artists are supposed to be men and women of courage and action, not cowards hiding in the shadows for fear of being attacked by fraudulent organizations and malicious trolls masquerading as true martial artists. The same thing that is happening in the martial arts world is happening in our country as a whole, just on a bigger scale.

Anyone who speaks out against certain practices or beliefs are now regularly attacked and silenced in our country. There is example after example of certain groups being silenced on social media. Certain speakers are routinely shouted down and silenced on college campuses today. If you support a political candidate who is hated by powerful people in Hollywood or celebrities, they attack your character in an attempt to discredit or marginalize you and your views.

These are the same tactics used by those who are using the martial arts for nothing other than their own dishonest purposes. I have seen them use these tactics time and time again. I am willing to bet that, if you have been in the martial arts for a long time, you have witnessed these people use these same tactics as well. It is disgraceful!

Many believe that having a governing body would solve this problem, but that would be an almost impossible task, especially since many of the frauds have risen to powerful positions in the martial arts world themselves and would probably be able to con their way into any governing body meant to reign over the martial arts community. We would most likely have the mental patients running the asylum and that would only make things worse.

This is why it is so important to keep your garden weeded. Once the weeds take over the garden, it is extremely hard to regain control and get things back to the way they once were.

Other factors have also played a part in the deterioration of the martial arts. Our culture has become extremely sue happy. Because of this, martial arts instructors have naturally had to take steps to protect themselves against being sued by some student or parent. This is one of the major reasons that the martial arts have been watered down.

Originally, martial arts were brutal. Bumps, bruises, and injuries were common place. Even sparring in practice sessions could be brutal at times. Now, if someone gets injured or hit too hard, there is always some sleazy lawyer who is willing to file a law suit for the parent or student.

Many instructors see this as an unnecessary risk and simply prefer to not teach certain techniques or to teach students to be overly controlled during sparring sessions. This is done to the point that the sparring sessions are not even real. Hey, at least nobody is getting sued that way, right?

Then we have the issue of politics in the martial arts world. I spent some time as a page for a representative in the Mississippi House of Representatives when I was younger, and I got to see firsthand how dirty politics truly are. That was almost 40 years ago, and as most of you would agree, politics have only gotten worse and worse since then.

Political posturing and fighting between the political parties in our country are doing more damage to our country than any outside enemy could possibly do. Abraham Lincoln stated, "America will never be destroyed from the outside. If we lose our freedoms it will be because we have destroyed ourselves from within." And this is what I see happening in our country and in the martial arts world today. We are allowing traditional martial arts and warrior ideals to be slowly forgotten, as martial artists are more focused on sporting events and hollow appearances.

True martial artists have allowed the martial arts to be watered down for the sake of political correctness and financial gain. We have allowed frauds and those with malicious intentions to run amuck, causing havoc throughout the martial arts world. We have allowed martial arts politics to dictate what is and isn't allowed in the martial arts world.

The truth is that martial arts politics are as dirty and underhanded as politics in Washington D. C. ever thought about being. There is very little loyalty left in the martial arts world. The majority of today's martial artists hold their finger up to see which way the political winds are blowing before they take a stand on anything.

If that wind is blowing against you, you can be fairly sure that the majority of these people will turn their back on you faster than they will drop a hot potato. Sifu Al Dacascos and I have had several conversations about the lack of loyalty and allegiance in the martial arts world.

I can't tell you how many martial arts instructors have told me about one of their students who they trained for years and years, who, when offered a rank promotion if he would turn his back on his instructor and start training with someone else, did so with no hesitation. This happens more often than you might think. Where is the loyalty and integrity in such an action?

Some underhanded federation and dishonest instructor who needs higher ranking students will simply poach students from other instructors and give them a rank promotion as if he trained this student through the rank of 7th dan or whatever it may be. This is not only dishonest politics, but shows a lack of respect and loyalty to both the student's instructor and the martial arts as a whole, but I have heard of this happening over and over again.

Political maneuvering is rampant throughout the martial arts world. It can be seen in the fake martial arts halls of fame, in dishonest instructors poaching students from other instructors, in the maneuvering between martial arts federations, and in blackballing independent martial artists from certain events, etc.

When you combine dishonest politics, shady practices and political correctness, you have a very bad combination, and the perfect conditions for the weeds to take over the garden. Add to those factors the fact that real martial artists are too busy training and working to improve their own lives to be bothered with the fools who are using the martial arts for their own dishonest gain, and you can easily see how the martial arts have deteriorated into what they have now become in many places.

And, if you are a martial artist and think that you are somehow above all of this stuff affecting you, think again. I have seen these political hacks and dishonest frauds attack and cause problems for even the most respected martial artists in the world today. If these people will attack martial artists such as Sifu Al Dacascos, Master Dana Abbott, and others, it is foolish to think that they will never target you.

This leaves us with only one question, "What can we do to save the martial arts and bring back the warrior ideals which the arts were founded on?" I will address this question in the next chapter.

It is not only what we do,
but what we do not do,
for which we are accountable.
Moliere

Chapter 13
Saving Traditional Martial Arts

*Complaining about a problem without
posing a solution is called whining.*
Teddy Roosevelt

I have exposed a lot of issues with today's martial arts community, not because I wanted to disparage, ridicule or criticize the martial arts, but to awaken those who were not aware of these problems, to warn martial artists, parents, and potential students, and to nudge those who are already aware of these problems to stand up and start to correct these issues.

I have been a martial artist for almost 35 years now. I have seen the issues which I discuss in this book firsthand. I have been conned by some of the martial arts halls of fame and some fake federations. I have seen dishonest martial arts cliques attack others and have had to deal with their attacks personally.

I have witnessed, firsthand, martial artists who have either bought, traded for, or promoted themselves to ranks that they did not earn. I have seen respected martial artists who allowed their egos to get the best of them and have sold their honor for 30 pieces of silver. I have seen McDojos which screw students and parents over with ridiculous contracts and fake credentials.

I have seen martial artists who claim to have worn out a dozen black belts, but who never tell you that they used sandpaper or their Maytag to wear out their belt. I have seen people get belt rank in Tae Kwon Do from people who never practiced Tae Kwon Do. I have seen people who claim to be Kajukenbo grandmasters who have never practiced Kajukenbo. I have seen people put into the martial arts hall of fame who were not even martial artists or even a black belt.

I haven't made up any of the problems which are hurting the arts which we all love; rather, I have witnessed each of these issues firsthand. I have seen how these people operate, how they con others, and how they profit from their dishonest practices. I have seen the dirty politics played out throughout the martial arts "good ole boy club."

Moreover, I have seen and been blessed to know many of the best martial artists in the world, and I am honored to call many of them my friends. I have discussed these issues at length with many of them, and they have seen and complained about the exact same issues that I have discussed in this book.

The problems are obvious; the solution is more complicated. But, as Teddy Roosevelt, a man's man who always walked his walk and never beat around the bush, stated, complaining about a problem without posing a solution is called whining. So in this chapter, I will pose several solutions to help get these issues under control and to help us stop the fraudulent and malicious martial artists who are a big part of the problem.

What can we, as martial artists, do to slow down or put an end to the dishonest practices which are growing at a rapid pace in the martial arts world? Can we really do anything to stop or curtail those who would use the martial arts in a dishonest way to take advantage of the unsuspecting or to fraudulently advance their own agendas?

Those are the million dollar questions. It seems that most martial artists have been content to simply look the other way or to simply ignore the actions of these dishonorable people. After all, much of what these people are doing is not against any laws. You can't legislate morals, although many have tried over the years.

There is no governing body for the martial arts world; everyone is free to claim they are a martial arts master, open up a McDojo, and start teaching "martial arts." I have heard many martial artists debate whether or not the martial arts community should have a governing body, but no one seems to be able to come to any consensus about this subject; and as a result, the status quo simply continues.

The first step in addressing the problems confronting the martial arts is for legitimate martial artists to care enough to take a stand against these fraudulent practices. I have talked to many martial artists about these problems, but not many are willing to stand up against those who are using the martial arts fraudulently.

They have many reasons for not wanting to get involved, but the main reason seems to be that once you take a stand for what is right, you become a target of these malicious frauds. They will use many of the underhanded tactics discussed in this book to try to discredit you or to destroy your reputation. Thus, it is easier, and safer, for legitimate martial artists to merely keep their heads down, look the other way, and go about their own business, hoping that they never become a target of those unscrupulous martial artists.

But nothing is gained by playing it safe. Great change rarely comes without risks. Until legitimate martial artists care enough to stand against unprincipled martial artists, these underhanded practices will continue. This said, there are ways that true martial artists can stand against these people without risking too much blowback or all of the personal attacks.

First, we should stop supporting the martial arts hall of fame scams. If you cut off their money and support, these dishonest businesses will disappear as quickly as they appeared, and they will become a thing of the past. But you must be willing to stop supporting them.

When they advertise their upcoming events, complete with the list of martial arts celebrities who are being paid to give the event some semblance of legitimacy, don't respond. Don't give them any likes or publicity on your social media profiles. Don't allow yourself to be wowed by their slick marketing skills.

When they send you that invitation to be "inducted" into their martial arts hall of fame (if you will pay them $250), turn it down. I get these invitations in the mail all the time, and they now go straight to the trash. When I get a personal invitation, I tactfully turn them down. Yes, I said "tactfully." Remember, respect and courtesy are two of the foundations of the martial arts. There is no reason to be rude and make enemies unnecessarily. Just say, "I appreciate it, but I am going to have to pass."

To do this, you must keep your ego in check. It can initially be a very good feeling to have someone contact you and say that he wants to induct you into the martial arts hall of fame. After all, you have given years and years to your training. You have worked through injuries, blood, sweat, and tears. It is all too easy to think to yourself, "Yeah, I do deserve this," and fall for the scam.

But remember, if they are asking you to *pay* for the privilege of being "inducted" into their hall of fame, you are *buying* your hall of fame induction, not *being* inducted. They are selling you a product, not honoring you with an induction. There is a huge difference!

You must consciously remind yourself that these businesses, and that is exactly what they are, businesses, are nothing more than a scam which seeks to prey on your ego. Resist the temptation to give in to your ego, and instead, stand on your honor and integrity. Knowing that your honor is intact is a much better feeling than paying for some cheap trophy!

Once enough legitimate martial artists refuse to take part in these scam hall of fame events, they will slowly start to disappear. This is the way of business. If they are not making money or getting some other perks from their business, they will close their doors. Of course, this won't happen overnight, but it will happen if enough of us stop supporting them.

The next step is very closely related to the first. We must quit treating martial arts frauds as if they are true martial artists. Yes, respect is important in the martial arts. Some might even say that respect is one of the cornerstones of the martial arts. But we must realize that there is a difference between *treating* someone with respect and *actually respecting* someone.

You should treat everyone with respect, at least until they have proven that they are not deserving of your respect. But that is completely different from giving true respect to frauds and con artists. Respect should be earned, not given out randomly. These people are not deserving of true respect and should not be given the same respect as real martial artists.

Do you have respect for the con artist on Wall Street who cons people out of millions of dollars? Of course not! Then why should you respect a con artist in the martial arts or the martial arts frauds who use the arts to con others out of their money in one way or another? The answer is simple – you shouldn't.

When you give these frauds, con artists, and borderline crooks the same respect that you give to legitimate martial arts masters, then you diminish that respect. Think about it. Do you have the same amount of respect for someone who has fraudulently purchased their belt rank and title, as you have for someone like Sifu Al Dacascos or Grandmaster Fumio Demura? Of course not! Why would you?

I constantly see martial artists giving respect to dishonest martial artists as if they are on the same level as true martial arts masters. This is what they wanted all along; this is why they paid big money for their fake belt rank and title. This is why they set up their fake martial arts halls of fame or started their own federation. They want the respect that goes along with earning their rank and title, but without putting in the work that it takes to actually *earn* that rank and title. Don't give it to them!

When you know that someone is a fraudulent martial artist, treat him as such. Ostracize him! Don't pose for pictures with him, knowing that he is going to use those photos for his underhanded marketing campaigns. Don't play into his hands.

Many martial artists claim that they don't want to do this because they don't want to make waves. They like going to the events because it is a time where they can get together with friends. Well, this may surprise you, but you can get together with your friends without paying some third rate hack for another cheap hall of fame trophy. True change always requires sacrifice of one kind or another. If you are not willing to deal with some short-term pain or sacrifice, there will be no long-term rewards. If you are not willing to forego another meaningless trophy, you simply do not care!

You didn't achieve your martial arts skills overnight; it took years and years of hard work and sacrifice. Likewise, these problems in the martial arts world are not going to go away without some sacrifice and the courage to stand for what's right. Taking the easy way out has never stopped a bully from bullying others; you have to overcome your fear and stand up to the bullies, or in this case, the frauds, the con artists, and the martial arts cliques.

Next, we have to remove politics from the martial arts community. Many of these martial arts cliques have grown strong because of their connections and the politics that they play. True martial artists are not interested in political games or underhanded backbiting; they just want to train, learn, and improve themselves.

But we have to realize that there are many others who spend an enormous amount of time playing political games, maneuvering to hurt other martial artists who they dislike or who they are in competition with, and vying for control in one way or another. Some of these people don't even train at all. They simply enjoy the drama and get a rush from trying to destroy others. This is not the way of the warrior or true martial artist!

Earning rank or martial arts titles should not depend on who you know or who you are friends with; they should actually be *earned*. What a novel idea – actually earning your belt rank! Too many people are getting rank advancements because of their connections, not their abilities or training. When everyone gets a black belt, the black belt no longer carries any meaning. This is especially true when people are being awarded black belts and they can't even fight their way out of a wet paper bag!

We need to remove politics from the martial arts world. We must stop competing against each other and start teaching each other and learning from each other. The martial arts should be a brotherhood, not a bunch of warring clans.

Maybe we should actually consider having some kind of governing body for the martial arts community. I am not talking about getting our incompetent government involved in the martial arts; God forbid that ever happens! But if we had some governing body which is set up to verify training, keep records of black belts, provide instructor training, etc., it could be an invaluable resource for those who are seeking legitimate training, *if* it is done with honor and integrity.

Of course, anyone could still teach self-defense classes or martial arts classes, but the governing body would be there for people who want to ensure that they are getting their training from an authentic, well-respected martial artist. It would not take that much to accomplish this.

Memberships to the governing body would be dependent on the actual verification of one's training and maybe the completion of an instructor's course. Everyone can "teach" martial arts classes, but not everyone can *teach*. There is a difference between running classes and being a true teacher.

Think of it this way. There have been thousands and thousands of professional football players, many who were the best of the best; but very few of those players have what it takes to be a great coach. Having the skills is one thing; being able to successfully teach others those skills is something entirely different.

The same thing applies to the martial arts. There are hundreds of thousands of martial artists in the world, but not all of them have what it takes to be a great teacher. I have trained with some instructors who were simply going through the motions and some who were absolutely amazing teachers. I can personally tell you that training with a true master is nothing like training with some martial artist who simply wanted to open his own dojo.

Certified training courses from a centralized governing body, for those who qualify for the instruction, would really help rid the martial arts world of some of the frauds who open McDojos and prey on unsuspecting or unknowledgeable students and parents. This would be especially true if this governing body had an easy to navigate website in which perspective students could find an instructor or check the credentials of a perspective instructor.

You don't rid your lawn of dandelions overnight, and we won't be able to get rid of the "weeds" in the martial arts world overnight. It will take a lot of effort by the martial arts community as a whole. It will take dedication to what is right over what is personally profitable. It will take courage and backbone. And most importantly, it will take the vast majority of martial artists working together as one to restore the heart and soul of the martial arts.

We must get back to focusing on character, honor and integrity in the martial arts community. Once we make character, honor and integrity the cornerstone of the martial arts, those who fail to live with honor and integrity will soon be ostracized and will find no place in the martial arts world unless they change their ways.

If people will put honor first, they won't compromise their honor or integrity for a fake hall of fame award. They won't buy fake rank or fraudulent titles. They won't set up fraudulent martial arts federations to cross-promote each other. They won't participate in the vile gossip that the martial arts cliques so easily spread, and they won't associate with those who do. Soon, those who participate in such activities will be seen as outcasts.

When it comes right down to it, all of the problems in today's martial arts world boils down to the love of money and overblown egos. People who put honor and integrity first place in their lives will never put what is personally profitable above what is right. They won't sell their honor for some bogus award, for a few dollars, or to satisfy their ego.

People who put character, honor and integrity first place in their life, always put what is right above everything else. If we want to stop the deterioration of the martial arts, we must take the perfection of our character seriously. We must teach our students to live with honor and integrity. We must refuse to associate or support those martial artists who act dishonorably.

It is not easy to stand up against those who are lowering their standards to make an easy buck or who are defrauding people throughout the martial arts world. When I write about such things, people inevitably write me and say, "That's easier said than done." Well, I have news for you. *Everything* is easier said than done!

If you want something for nothing, martial arts is not the place for you. Martial arts builds character because you have to work hard to become what you want to be. You don't develop martial arts skills by dreaming about becoming Bruce Lee; you develop your martial arts skills through hard work, persistence, patience, and determination. It takes a lot of work, time and effort. You don't get anything worthwhile by taking the easy road.

Yes, you may make some enemies when you start standing up for what is right. Lord knows I have made many enemies in the martial arts world because I dare to speak my mind and state the truth. I am sure that there will be many more who start attacking me after writing this book and exposing their dark secrets. So be it!

God did not put me on this planet to suck up to men and women of low character. It is not my goal in life to have everyone like me. If my telling the truth rubs you the wrong way, maybe you have some soul searching to do. I do what is mine to do and let the chips fall where they may.

This is the attitude that all true martial artists must develop if we are to have any chance of getting the martial arts world back to what it should be. You can't walk in honor and integrity, while at the same time, associating with frauds, con men, and scam artists in order to stay on their good side. As the Bible teaches, "What fellowship does light have with darkness?" It is time to stand against the darkness and shine the spotlight on those who would twist the martial arts to achieve their dishonest objectives.

Until the vast majority of true martial artists are determined to stand up against the frauds, the con artists, and those who do not conduct themselves with honor and integrity, nothing will change. The bully never changes his ways simply because he wakes up one day with a change of heart; someone must stand up to him and give him a hard core attitude adjustment.

It is time for all serious martial artists to stand together and denounce those who are making a mockery of the martial arts, or at the very least, to stop supporting their scams, frauds, and malicious lies and gossip. It is time to start choosing your friends more carefully and to re-evaluate some of those who have entered our lives as martial artists.

First, get *your* own life in order. Make sure *you* are living with honor and integrity. Focus on improving *your* character daily. Work to perfect *your* character, as Master Funakoshi taught. Then stop entertaining those who you know to be frauds and scam artists; just send them packing.

Once you have made the necessary adjustments in *your* life, then teach your students and friends to do the same. We change the martial arts by changing minds, one person at a time, and one dojo at a time.

If we will all take our part seriously, soon we will start to see those who continue to support fraudulent martial arts halls of fame and scam federations, those who fake their credentials, those with ego problems, and the cliques who love to gossip and trash the reputations of other martial artists, start to be ostracized to the point that they will start disappearing from the martial arts world altogether. Here are 10 things we need to do, or to stop doing, in order to make changes in the martial arts world.

The 10 Things we need to do to Change the Martial Arts World

1) Refuse to accept any award or hall of fame trophy for which you have to *pay*. If you are paying for it, it is not a hall of fame induction; it is only you buying yourself a little trophy to market yourself.

2) Quit supporting those people who run the scam martial arts halls of fame. Without the support of other martial artists, these people will have to close their doors for good and only the legitimate martial arts halls of fame will remain.

3) If you know of someone who has bought their belt rank, cross-promoted each other to a high rank, or self-promoted himself to a high rank, call them out and cut them off. They

are liars and con artists and should be exposed for what they are. Their actions need to have consequences. Remember, stating the truth is not the same thing as gossiping.

4) Keep your ego in check and make sure that you teach your students to do the same. The fake halls of fame and fraudulent federations only persist because of people whose egos are more developed than their martial arts skills.

5) Refuse to gossip, or to listen to gossip, about other martial artists. The malicious martial arts cliques are only able to control people and parts of the martial arts world because people are willing to listen to their gossip and to repeat gossip about other true martial artists. Always consider the source and dig deeper for the truth.

6) Teach your students true martial arts, not what passes for martial arts in most dojos today. Don't compromise the essence of your martial art in order to make it fit into todays silly idea of what the martial arts should be. This is especially true if you are going to participate in martial arts tournaments where so much of the martial arts have been bastardized.

7) Never put money or marketing above your honor and integrity! The love of money is the root of all evil, and plays a large roll in what has gone wrong in the martial arts world. Keep your priorities straight!

8) Make sure you take the time to teach character training to your students. Teach them what it means to live with honor, integrity and courage by being a good example for them to follow. This means you must stand for what is right at all times. They will be watching how you conduct yourself; your example is more important than you realize.

9) Make sure you are teaching the warrior mindset to your students, not just martial arts techniques. The warrior mindset is vital to all martial arts students. Everyone needs a code to live by, and everyone needs to be taught about the traits

which should be in their code. As Confucius said, "I am not one who was born with great wisdom. I love the ancients and diligently seek wisdom among them." Even Confucius has to be taught the ways of the sage.

10) Develop the courage to stand up for what is right. It takes courage to not go along with something that most everyone else is going along with. It is not easy. You must conquer your fear of being disliked or of being attacked, and simply stand for what is right. Always remember the great truism, a little bit of light pushes away a lot of darkness.

The only thing necessary for the
triumph of evil is for good men to do nothing.
Edmund Burke

The Man in the Glass

When you get what you want in your struggle for pelf,
And the world makes you king for a day,
Then go to the mirror and look at yourself,
And see what that man has to say.

For it isn't your father, or mother, or wife,
Who judgement upon you must pass.
The fellow whose verdict counts most in your life
Is the man staring back from the glass.

He's the fellow to please, never mind all the rest,
For he's with you clear up to the end,
And you've passed your most dangerous, difficult test
If the man in the glass is your friend.

You may be like Jack Horner and "chisel" a plum,
And think you're a wonderful guy,
But the man in the glass says you're only a bum
If you can't look him straight in the eye.

You can fool the whole world down the pathway of years,
And get pats on the back as you pass,
But your final reward will be heartaches and tears
If you've cheated the man in the glass.

Peter Dale Wimbrow, Sr.

About Dr. Bohdi Sanders

Dr. Bohdi Sanders is a multi-award winning and bestselling author. His books, *Modern Bushido: Living a Life of Excellence* and *Men of the Code*, both hit #1 on Amazon. Seven of his other books have also been best-sellers and were also ranked in the Top 10 on Amazon. Dr. Sanders has been a martial artist for over 34 years and has trained in Shotokan Karate, Krav Maga, and Escrima with noted martial artists Master Bob Allen, Shihan William Jackson, and Sifu Al Dacascos. Dr. Sanders is a 5th degree black belt in Shotokan Karate. His work has won several national book awards and has reached martial artists throughout the world. He is the author of:

- *Modern Bushido: Living a Life of Excellence*
- *Men of the Code: Living as a Superior Man*
- *Warrior: The Way of Warriorhood*
- *BUSHIDO: The Way of the Warrior*
- *Defensive Living: The Other Side of Self-Defense*
- *The Warrior Lifestyle*
- *Wisdom of the Elders*
- *Secrets of the Martial Arts Masters*

Dr. Sanders' books have received high praise and he has won several national awards, including:

- #1 New Release on Amazon.com: Secrets of the MA Masters 2018
- #1 Bestseller Amazon.com: Men of the Code 2015
- #1 Bestseller Amazon.com: *Modern Bushido* 2013
- The Indie Excellence Book Awards: 1st Place Winner 2013
- USA Book News Best Books of 2013: 1st Place Winner 2013
- The Indie Excellence Book Awards: 1st Place Winner 2010
- USA Book News Best Books of 2010: 1st Place Winner 2010

Other books from Kaizen Quest Publishing

9 781937 884246